My Marianismo:
Nurturing Myself from the Roots to the Bloom

by
Cynthia Alonzo Perez

Foreward by
Sofia Mendoza

Author Contributions from
Emely Rumble
Mayra Najera
Rosa Shetty
Irelia Ozaeta
Angelia Santiago
Veronica Rodriguez-Cabrera

Thank you to the authors of this garden of apapachos as an offering for the collective .

Foreword by Sofia Mendoza, LCSW

I am honored to write the foreword for "My Marianismo: A decolonial love story about blossoming into our legacy" because it is exactly that. A love letter to herself, as I have had the privilege of knowing Cynthia as a friend, comadre, colega and maestra. Several years back, I committed to my own continuous healing journey in the form of writing, creativity, reading, and taking in others' medicinas. Since then, I've attended most of Cynthia's Courses rooted in inner child, generational trauma, and decolonial perspectives in healing. It has made me a more nurturing adult to my inner nina, a more attuned mom, and the holistic therapist my clients deserve.

From the moment I was introduced to this book, My Marianismo: Nurturing Myself from the Roots to the Bloom, I knew it was something special. This book is a tender gift to the world. "My Marianismo" is grounded in a blend of ancestral wisdom, modern psychological practices, and a deep understanding of complex trauma and healing. This is Cynthia's wheelhouse. Her expertise lies in guiding individuals through the healing of intergenerational wounds, particularly through inner child work and the deconstruction of Marianismo, a traditional concept of female roles and identity within Latinx cultures.

My Marianismo touches on tough topics that include the harm caused by trauma, racism, white supremacy, traditional gender roles while at the same time, offering nurturing guidance on how to heal by co-regulating with your inner child, the elements, our well-ancestors, our senses, and our joy – all in the present moment. Know that you'll be held by the compassionate words and exercises on the pages.

Cynthia has always been a dynamic speaker, writer and presenter and you will see this throughout the book. You will find yourself relating to parts of her story, making connections to your own history, craving to center your self-care as a crucial pillar to your legacy and find meaningful ways to "move the needle" on your healing process.

I wholeheartedly recommend this book to anyone who is on a mission to break free from intergenerational expectations, unburden themselves, and reclaim joy and healing. See this as your tender tool-kit for self healing and liberation.

With all my love,
Sofia Mendoza, LCSW

www.sofiamendozalcsw.com
www.mendingrootshealingspaces.com

Loving Acknowledgement

This could not be without my partner, Mike. I couldn't have seen these sides of myself with out his constant love and encouragement of me.

I realize my parents didn't get to have this kind of safety with each other as they were both always critical of each other and what I have in my partnership is a friendship and mutual effort to show love and care for one another.

I realize it's my privilege to get to live a rich authentic full life and not just GIVE love, but receive it. Being with Mike I have been able to feel love without pushing it away or humbling myself to feel undeserving. I feel safe, seen, and accepted and that is My Marianismo legacy to disfrutar.

To Idris, Miles and Malcolm, thank you for allowing me so many opportunities to play.

A note for the adult children of Marianistas

This book is for you, for us. Thank you for giving me a space to learn, unlearn and experience, omg the experiences I have had with my own mother during this 5 year deep dive into MY MARIANISMO. This book is for the people whom have attended my Rooted in Reflection or WellMamaCafe events in the past. You and us, we have felt the gentle energy of our own inner child's forgiveness and shared our Marianismo unravelings together. I remember speaking at Cal State LA on Epigenetics and Marianismo and the crowd was so diverse and the men had so much to add to this conversation. This is for those children who feel their mother is ashamed of them for not being like so and so's daughter. I hope you see it is not your job to make her see your magic, it's your job to pursue yourself and spread the magic you learn of your own light to the collective and to your mother in whatever amount is in your field to give at the moment. This is for us first gens reclaiming our indigenous medicine and through this we have created communities of healers that are willing to share how they started their business or who can provide reiki services as community resources. We are re-building a social network of re-parenting our ancestral inner child. Imagine if we let them grow in their indigenous magic and kept all the goodness of their people's land and ceremony and remembered by living it. By softening to it. By being a witness of what would once be called conceited by white supremacy is now called self-love; which is a basic human need. Self-love, as a daughter of immigrants, was not humble enough, it was not giving "sacrifice things like self-enjoyment, pon te a limpiar".

Through talking to you and others like you, I have met so many inspiring people who resonate with Marianismo wounds and the delicate balance of being a change maker but also carrying guilt for setting limits or resting. I had an event at Casita Bookstore in Long Beach, CA in 2022 called "Love Letters to My Inner Child" and we journaled and did an inner child guided visualization and platica. There were only 5 people who arrived and wouldn't you know it? It was exactly the 5 for me. Two of them hired me for private wellness events and I got to lead guided visualizations and hold space with the group in whimsical and vulnerable experiences. And it has been magical. I GET to talk about Marianismo, with you, and them, and it makes it easier for me to remember my own value and set the pace we know we deserve. Thank you to the people who joined the Re-Parenting My Inner Child with Joy groups from 2021-2024. What a beautiful time in life that was mirroring the collective shift. I was able to host 16 cohorts of people wanting to love on their inner child. Thank you to those who let me "pilot" My Marianismo Platicas! I want to say thank you to Esther, Tina, Maria, Nikolai, Emely, Ceci, Sofia, Amanda, Claribel, Karla, Lydiana, Natalie, and anyone else I forgot for letting me go off on these "theories" and "visions". Thank you for your consejos and kindness while I navigate this Marianismo journey in REAL TIME. I hope we are moving forward what is our Soul's highest good and leaving the rest for everyone to claim their part in. I hope we give back in ways that elevate the collective heart and for liberation all people, all lands.

Disclaimer:

This book was written with love for you and me and the next generations.
This serves as an invitation to notice what comes up within you while reading and reflecting on your own lineage.

I also ask you to notice what you notice.
There will likely be errors in this book. Do mistakes feel uncomfortable for you? Does it remind you of your own humanity? Perspective can be our narrative to reclaim.

You see, I had to get this book out. My ancestors have let me know this in many ways. And the biggest thing I finally did is let go of the colonial expectation of perfectionism. The reality is I am a 40year old mom of 3 who is learning through homeschooling and being a mom to a new college student. I am this book's author, spiritual connection, space holder, editor, publisher, marketer and biggest cheerleader. I work as a Manager of Behavioral Health at the moment and supervise clinicians form a de-colonial perspective as best I can in a healthcare system.I am also a business owner of Rooted in Reflection, a wellness agency which creates soft spaces for epigenetic healing. I am the host of the podcast Confetti All Around, and a neurodivergent creative who loves to write and make up whimsical frameworks through research and ancestral stories.

I realized one day when I kept saying I cannot publish this book until I am paid with a signed contract by a major publisher. But the truth is, that may not happen. And it reminded me so much of my ancestors, so many roles, so many stories and remedies and traditions, disregarded, destroyed, diminished. And that made me look at all I do and say, the amount of time I have spent preserving this framework and weaving it with clinical suggestions is not just enough, it is innovative, it's de-colonial care, it's a paradigm shift. My friend Sofia Mendoza, LCSW is a clinical supervisor and owner of Mending Roots Healing Spaces. She has self-published over 35 workbooks for wellness and connection. Sofia's books are visibility in the mental health field in a space where no one was asking US. And yet we can do this and we do so much everyday and still don't think it's enough until it is asked for. Sofia inspired me to share my wisdom, experiences and medicinas with the world.

This is an invitation to put yourself on too. Share your stories. Step out of humility and into your magic. This is an invitation to indulge.

This book started as my own shadow work, after the inner child healing I opened this door to my mother wounds. This marianismo mother wound is vast and vastly under researched in mental health. Academia mentions it but it requires research and scientific variables to quantify our stories, our oral histories and our genetic cosmology. However, our stories matter always.

This book has contributions, offerings from living ancestors in the the shape of everyday women and in the craft of authors today and healers tonight. They are rooted in collective love and healing the mother wound with plants, land, and ancestor's conservation of wisdom. I am in deep gratitude of everyone who said yes to contributing to this book and the conversations that will ripple from this constellation of work.
Thank you deeply, from my ancestors to yours.

Que Pacho?

My mom would answer the house phone like that when my friends called. Correction, she would answer the phone saying, "Bueno", not like a question, like a statement, a pleasant acknowledgement of the ring. I would listen to her say hello *"bueno"* then observe her response and know who was on the phone by her next words, "oh hello" meant it was business or someone we did not know. But when someone we loved would call on the phone, she would reply to their greeting with the following words, *"Hola, que pacho? Que me cuentas?"* I loved these small intimate moments of witnessing my mother in her own personhood. Not being a mom or a wife or the daughter or a machista or marianista, just her, eager to chat with familiares and warm to the conversation. Que pacho is an affectionate way of asking Que Pasa? or Que Paso? It's a friendly Que Pacho.

I never realized how special those greetings were until my high school best friend Leslie said, " I love calling your house and chatting with your mom, it makes me feel special and she always says the same thing once I say hi, *Hola Leslie, que pacho*?!" It was once Leslie named it I realized, I too love those moments. I noticed my mom was calm, she was present, she was attentive to the response she was going to recieve. I loved seeing her sit at the kitchen dining table and twirl the white phone cord around her finger as she talked to her own mother and her mother would pass the phone around to her siblings and nephews to shout hello to her. She would get so excited to hear what everyone back home in Merida was doing. She would make me say hello and although I was always embaressed to say more than hello in my broken Spanish, I secretly loved when they were on the line, I knew my mom was happy. She would buy calling cards each week to talk to them and those calls were some of the happiest moments in her week. Sometimes they would call us while we were watching a TV Novela and I would hear my mom laugh and gossip about the novelas with her sister and then after 15 minutes or so they would say goodbye. I think that's another thing I loved about those calls, they would calm my mom's longing, if only for the evening. She would return to the couch where I was subtly eavesdropping while playing Sonic the Hedgehog on my Sega, and she would bring snacks like quesadillas or sliced fruit and spend time with me. It's almost like once she felt held and seen by her family, she could come back and witness me.

I loved when I would call her as an adult and she would answer her cell phone with *que pacho* and I would just know that was my cue, I could cry, vent or invite her and in that moment, she was available for me.

While I finish this book I am not on the best terms with my own mother, while it is more than complicated, she has end stage liver disease due to sheer lifelong stress. Her mood has changed & her surpressed trauma has resurfaced. This is a longer story but the gist of it is what I would give to call my mom and feel her warm presence say to me, *Hola hija, que pacho*, and mean it.

This book is dedicated to the mothers, fathers, and children of Palestine. As this book was written we are almost a year into the violence and systematic torture and eradication of Palestinian culture, traditions, lands and lineages. Every day my body remembers them and moves through various survival feelings. What is happening in Gaza is related to the same roots of Colonialism of Marianismo and our bones know the story of our brothers and sisters in Gaza. I hope by the time you read this book the United States has stopped sending weapons and sanctions have been imposed to preserve life and land in Gaza back to its descendants and liberate Gaza indefinitely.

Understanding Epigenetics and Marianismo is supportive maternal mental health care for Latine/Xicane/Diaspora parents and children.

Understanding Epigenetics and Marianismo is Liberation from the heavy burden to fawn or flee.

Understanding Epigenetics and Marianismo is being present with our mother's grief and our own inner child's needs.

Understanding Epigenetics and Marianismo is seeing your mother's inner child raised along side you.

Understanding Epigenetics and Marianismo is Liberation for sons who carry the heavy burden of gender roles instilled by their mother

Understanding Epigenetics and Marianismo is liberation of 14 generations in our genes carrying the heavy burden of gender roles and colonialism.

The foundation of this framework

So just to give you a little bit of history on why I gotta do this like this, I've been consulted, *why don't you just call it mother wounds? Why don't you just focus on inner child healing?* I thank inner child healing for so much of my softening and my creativity in my business. I thank her for showing me what I am capable of when free to be as I am and more. I still believe inner child work is my core strength and marianismo is the shadow ancestral work. That's why I also provide "sacred vessels", a hammock homecoming ceremony on the land and under the trees. It is probably my most intimate ceremonies I offer. My loving inner mother is only as gentle as I am with my marianismo.

There has just always been something about me that I kept coming back to and that was, I cannot not highlight what I see here that no one has expanded on. So with Rooted in Reflection, I focused on *marianismo and epigenetics*. In these last three years, I will say, I have been led to the research using book divination, bibliomancy, as I learned from my favorite bibliotherapist Emely Rumble, LCSW Founder of Literapy.

I've been led to Marianismo in unexpected ways and I couldn't understand why. Why do I feel this strong urge to talk about it? While my bachelor's degree is actually in Chicano Latino studies, my parents, immigrants of Yucatan were like, "why? Why are we paying for you to go to college, The American dream...We're so proud. Why are you majoring in Chicano Studies? Just to learn how to be Mexican?" And I was like, no, I'm just, I'm fascinated by the history. I love social justice and something's calling me. And I remember it was in that Chicano Studies program at Cal State Long Beach that I heard the word **Marianismo** for the first time. And of course we spent only one day discussing it.

But I was like, how come we don't talk about this more? Marianismo, why do we not talk about it and the implications on our mental and physical health as we uphold it? Because we focus more on the work of the men and the great achievements, but also how women helped the men gain rights. Cue the The Chicano Movement. So that little part of Marianismo ever since then always stuck by me. And then 15 years later, here I am creating workshops, continuing education courses, and trainings on *"Marianismo and Epigenetics: Using our Ancestral Knowing to Heal Legacy Wounds"*.

But it wouldn't be until this year, just three months ago, I took a genealogy test and I found out that my lineage up to the 1600s are from Mani, el Pueblo Magico de Mani, Yucatan.

I knew this, but I didn't really soak it in. See, because my family lives in Merida, Yucatan. They have also live near the beaches of Merida, Campeche, Chichxulub, and Progreso. And so these are the places I've always heard about. And I heard about Mani, but I was like, well, who cares? And then when I found this out, it meant so much.

I invite you to read about Mani at pueblosmagicostrenmaya .com.

What is Marianismo?

The term "Marianismo" was coined in 1973 by political scientist Evelyn Stevens in her essay "Marianismo: The Other Face of Machismo". The term is used to describe the gender-based expectations for women in Latin American society, and is thought to have originated during the Spanish conquest. It comes from the Spanish word María, which refers to the Virgin Mary, and is intended as the female counterpart to machismo, the Hispanic ideal of masculinity.

Rooted in Catholicism and colonialism, it is a social construct created out of a caste system of gender and status.
Women were taught to be like the Virgin Mary and sacrifice for the man and the community. This shifted the natural flow of energy in their bodies to survive colonialism. This has become energy that informs how we are with others and how we see the world.
This became a value, which became a belief, which became a behavior, a way of showing up. It has made women physically sick to hold all this without acknowledging what is theirs.

Marianismo represents the duality that womb holders have and the pressure that we have to be agreeable, to be helpful, to be all these facets. And it's important for us to think, okay, but we also have a bag of gems. I haven't been in that bag yet. Let's start to bring out that bag and be in our duality. If we're always just in the doing and the stressing, we're not really experiencing all of our legacy resources. So these legacy burdens, they're rooted in survival and due to oppression, they push conformity and they push social constructs to protect the lineage. It's trying to be helpful, but it is also pushing, you know, social norms.

Please note, this book is written from a de-colonial approach whereas Catholicism's teaching are the beginning of colonial dogma. This framework is not to disrespect the role of the Virgin Mary but actually acknowledge how she too is a victim of gender constructs that has stripped her of a legacy deserving of human fallacy and intimacy with others out of fear of falling off the pedestal. This is an invitation to ground in our authentic human purpose as a divine living ancestor.

My Marianismo roots

Being in my marianismo resources, I am re-wiring my brain to remember my ancestor's medicine and knowledge. I have felt my sacral cells open as I expand my window of tolerance with expansive creativity and child like joy. I find myself noticing the moment I choose to be softer, more present. I notice when I am kind to myself, I am available to receive kindness and be transparent. I naturally start to raise my children with this grace. And even if I didn't have children, if I'm a teacher, if I'm around children, I'm a bedside nurse, I'm a neighbor, right? We are going to be impacting those with our energy. So what ways do we want to protect and strengthen these little magical epigenetic cellular reminders of who we are? How can we pull those out and want to show up with this, this talent right here.

I recommend inner child healing. With rituals from our inner creator, we can love on our inner child with more ease. With inner child healing, mother wounds reveal themselves.

Marianismo awareness in many ways is our ancestral shadow work. It works almost in the opposite way of inner child healing. With inner child healing I usually start fun and playful then we go deep to all the feelings. In Marianismo work we start at the roots, in the deep. We get to then acknowledge and understand the roots and watch ourselves blossom. The rose bloom is worth the journey and grows abundantly. It is cultivated and nurtured once the roots are tended to.

Maybe it starts small and we like really just finesse it and in communication with our ancestors we go, what do you have to show for me? And then we create safety for our body to show us, for our energy to show us. Just an invitation, just a little thought.

Thinking about my marianismo with awareness and compassion what does that look like? what does it look like to welcome marianismo with your awareness and compassion so i created this book. To hold a space for whose energy our bones carry.

The Epigenetic Impact of Marianismo

The epigenetic impact of marianismo is like confetti all around, within your cells and in your organs. As I sit here completing my fourth self-published book and probably my most proud and ancestor backed work, it is with mixed feelings. I guess I can call this moment a true "Confetti All Around" moment. I chose the title to my podcast for the imagery of the words, when confetti is tossed around it is usually in celebration of something. It is a happy moment. Until, it is time to clean up the mess, in which case the confetti is no longer a party decoration but trash, a mess. "Who is going to pick up this mess?" my dad would always say when I had a piñata or confetti. When my excitement would get "too big" he would bring it back down to earth with criticisms, scarcity and fear. The juxtaposition of this description is my first birthed son Miles .When he was 18 months old and his brother was a new born I was out of it, trying to muster up my instincts and calmness that felt lost in the wind. I carried a deep fear (ahem my epigenetic history of child deaths and mother abandonment was activated). I remember being so tired and in my fog but Miles used to say this statement with such joy at that age, "Confetti All Around!", how would shout while pumping his fist in the air. He was mimicking Luigi, his favorite Nintendo character. He was such a light when he did it that it would snap me out of the trance I was in, even if only for that moment. I saw his joy and his celebration. "Confetti All Around, what a duality, what a concept. The joy and the mess" I would remember writing in my journal.

Here I am now with 3 seasons of my podcast that I have enjoyed hosting. As the world has changed so much since I started, I know that podcast was divine timing.

While I have been transitioning jobs and roles, and being creatively expansive, shit has also been hitting the fan in my family in a way I would have never imagined. Honestly the details of this epocha needs it's own book but that's another day. I honestly can't believe everything that has gone on but what I will take from this horrible situation is the lesson in the story to share.

Throughout my new mother era, my relationship with my parents has ebbed and flow. I would say from 2016-2021 my parents helped me in the first 5 years of my kids life. Though now I regret the times I would be ungrateful or too strict with my parent's as caregivers, I now see how much love they gave my children. They really made all of their time about them, for them. I would work from my childhood bedroom upstairs in their home while my parents watched my kids downstairs. My dad would take them in the pool and be with them for hours as they played. My mom would watch them and make their snacks and meals. If my husband and I had a long week with little sleep, they would have the kids sleep over on Saturdays and my kids still miss those days where "gampa" made the perfect omelettes and pancakes and my mom bought them toys and treats. They would take us on vacations, my most memorable being a cruise where we had a memorable time together not realizing it would be the last trip together.

In winter of 2021, everything changed. My dad had been struggling with back issues for over a decade and had tried many solutions but ultimately nothing helped and he was growing increasingly agitated and irritable. His personality became unbearable sometimes because he was in so much pain and felt that he was doing an unfair share of the load at home. I should state that both of my parents were retired at this point and my brother was living at the house. My dad, a natural busy body and type A personality, was constantly bickering with my mom. It became so bad that they weren't sleeping in the same bedrooms and the kids started to feel the energy. That is when we started to express concern and limit our time with them.

Honestly, I always felt guilty if I went a whole week without visiting my parents home. I always worried about my mom's happiness but at the same time, she could never be happy for long, it's almost like she always gravitated to being miserable. She was never active or had hobbies besides shopping. Shopping is her disassociation. Shopping is a way to imagine a life she is not living but longing for. Shopping has been my mom's addiction and we just tolerated her hoarding of stuff from TJ Maxx because it seemed harmless, especially when compared to the drinking in our lineage. My mom's shopping was always an argument for my parents. My mom always tried to buy happiness, buy people's love. It was always enfuriating to me when I would ask her to meet an emotional need with her presence, her listening, her connection and thought she would try, her buying you a purse you didn't need or a toy your kids already have felt more manageable as a way of showing she thought of you. I remember Christmases she would buy herself all the things I said I wanted and I would have to sit and watch her open up the gifts to herself that she wrapped up. We would all pretend to be surprised as she opened her own gifts and acted like she didn't know that was the same sweater I had asked for. It was sad and annoying and yet I think we always just felt bad for her misery so much that we allowed her to guilt us and dictate the theatrics of the holiday.

In November 2022 my dad was finally approved for back surgery and my mom started to realize she would be his main caregiver after his 12 week recovery from back surgery. It was then that my mom started to tell me she didn't want to life the rest of her life with her husband, my dad. I listened, I have listened to these empty threats my whole life and many times yelled "then do it! Stop talking about it and do it!" because I was sick of her blaming her children for why she was still married and miserable. To my surprise, one week after my dad's back surgery, she got so angry and told my dad to leave. He called me worried about how wild she was acting. My dad is a loving big hearted guy but I also know how annoying and threatening he can be when angry. I asked him to pack his bag and head to Arizona with my big sister (also named Aurora) for the holiday and I would talk to my mom about her plans.

This problem between them has a long history before I was born. This resentment they each have is valid on both sides. My dad felt like he tried his whole marriage to make her happy. He worked hard, took care of the kids, he would drive us and pick us up from school and he was the responsible steady adult. He was loyal to my mother and always believed she would One day respond how he had imagined. He felt she always took her siblings and parent's side over his since they were dating. She would let her family borrow money and not return it, she would let them dictate her plans and she would always seem to want to be doing whatever their life was. My dad was always resentful of this and it did not bring out his best parts. He would make fun of her family, even in front of her siblings and their children. I would be so disgusted by my dad's behavior I would often yell at him. His dad was a very critical person who constantly used "jokes" to mask his deep sadness and grief. My mom had decided that at 71, she was sick of this way of living and wanted to try to be independent. She said the arguing was making her sick. He said he was always arguing with her because she never let him care for her and everything he did for her became "not good enough". I saw both sides and both of them often were living in the worst parts of themselves, for 45 years.

It was April 2023 and it had been five wild emotional months of my dad living in Arizona with my sister and my mom living in her home alone with my brother. Between then my mom spiraled several times with reoccurring childhood traumas and resentment about her marriage which she blamed had limited her. I honestly believe my mom's regret was her own anger at how her whole life was constant, daily, moment to moment self abandon so much that she didn't even know who she was, who she was coming home to. I had been helping my mom live without my dad by going over often with my kids and planning her medical appointments for her. I felt responsible for helping my mom sort out her life at 71 because I wasn't mad that she wanted to be single. Sure I worried greatly about my dad's emotional and physical state (he had a TIA mini stroke in Arizona that same month due to the stress) but knew my sister was the best person to care for him. I tell them he went from one Aurora to the next. My dad had helped my sister through her difficult divorce and now she got to support my dad and heal her oldest daughter rekindles with the eldest son father wounds. My mom when left alone to her own devices was unable to manage her finances, her schedule, buying groceries, paying her bills, everything my dad took care of started to show itself. She had felt her life had become like her mothers. While I don't know how much is now intertwined as her memory or her mom's the imprint of trauma started to surface stronger every month she was single. She started unburying deep sacred anger towards her father for how he treated her mother and the pain she felt seeing her mom suffer with so much work and responsibility. My mom was grieving her long life living in different places than her mother and not being with her family.

My mom and I had visited Merida together with both of my sons and we had a wonderful time. She was finally opening up and telling me her stories. I then understood why she hadn't shared her stories with me before as I realized she had many memories of feeling distrusting of others, betrayed, and never good enough. She longed for love she didn't get as a child and she spent her whole life, my whole childhood and adult hood, trying to find it in buying things for people, in being everywhere she was invited and even places she wasn't invited to. She felt pulled in every direction often because I believe she didn't have her own inner compass, it had been so long since she knew herself she didn't know her own path. I have so much sadness as I remember knowing this part of my mother. I also feel very honored to have been gifted with this time and truth to see her own wounds and give my inner child the love she was not going to get from the mother that was also longing for this love.

In May 2023 my mother texted me to book her a plane ticket back home from Merida to her house in California. She was in urgency and set on the date. I didn't understand until she did arrive back home. "Hey, I think mom is involved with online scammers. She is behaving really weird since being back and I found these Apple gift cards and the receipts hidden in the couch. Should I be concerned?" my brother Marcel said. Knowing my mom's energy of quick to not trust someone, I replied, "I wouldn't be too concerned but maybe keep the cards, don't mention it to her and just keep an eye on her". I called her siblings and asked each of them if they knew if my mom had been talking to scammers. They all lied and said they had no idea. Later my aunt, her only sister, would admit that they all knew because she started talking to these online scammers on facebook while in Mexico. She said the siblings had tried to tell her to stop and they all got into an argument about Aurora's autonomy as the eldest sibling. My aunt said she and the siblings made a pact to never tell us and protect my mom's secret. This moment made me feel like I was deeply abandoned by my family, her family. I can say this moment would create a large scale wound in our lineage that this moment defined. My uncles in their own machismo believed that as the eldest, whatever my mom did was none of my business and I should leave her be out of "respect". One uncle said, "I don't care if your mom is homeless because she decided to give all her money to them, it is her life and her business". That of course did not sit well with me and if course I got into a cursing match via text with this uncle who would shortly after defraud her out of over $10,000 even so much as helping her take out a loan for "home repairs" with his realtor know how. Her other brother ignored my tears as I begged him to please help me with my mom and he too shut me out. And the other three brothers that might have helped me, well they had all died three years in a row of liver disease so I couldn't ask them but I have a feeling they would have supported me.

I believe my mom and her siblings have this deep trauma bond due to being left alone with each other as not just siblings that collectively miss their parents, but also as caretakers of eachother, they have always kept this pact of siblings over everyone else. This was so strong that I remember ten years ago I found my mother crying in her bed and when I asked why she was crying she told me her oldest brother had cancer for years and he had told her and her sister and made them promise not to tell his wife and children. My uncle's cancer was progressing and my mom felt alone in carrying this secret, this burden. I told her I think she should tell her brother to tell his children so that she has more support, so that they can be there for him. I'm not sure of the timeline but he had a long difficult battle with cancer due to substance use, stress and heck maybe even chemical exposure in the fields. He was a good brother to her, the two of them were the eldest and he was the first to die. That grief still takes my mothers breath away. Her two younger brothers would get diagnosed with cirrohsis of the liver shortly after that and died within one year of each other. I believe she never had safety to grieve this. I believe these loses activated her epigenetic grief from a long line of women before her who had grieved so many unfair circumstances.

My mom has been under the mental hack, the brainwashing of several online scammers since 2023 that she has deteriorated. We noticed she wasn't eating and doesn't cook anymore. She would wait for others to eat and eat a very tiny amount. The scammers live in another part of the world and call her like fake AI faces and she believes she is talking to a real person. Being a medical social worker myself I made her all the necessary appointments. I told the doctors everything how my mom has been in a massive amount of stress since leaving my dad, how she is lonely, how she has been scammed out of her pension monthly and how she believes this is a real person when it's a criminal enterprise. The doctors tried to help me as best they could but my mom was able to pass the MMSE and other memory tests yet was unable to open a cup of noodles or unlock her bedroom door. Upon further testing her doctor told us, "you have end stage liver disease called cirrohisis of the liver. It is in its end stages and will progress." My mom didn't seem to understand, how could she be diagnosed with the same illness her brothers and her dad had acquired when she herself did not drink. I insisted it was the diabetes and the constant insulin injections. I researched holistic liver disease and found it used to be called "non alcoholic fatty liver disease" caused by a build up of fat. Her liver specialist stated what could have advanced my mom's illness was a lifetime of toxic stress. They said toxic stress creates physical illness because it sends cortisol as energy to the bodies to fight/flight/flee and when we are constantly stressed and that cortisol is not released out of the body via movement, creation or expression, it becomes waste to our organs and my mom's liver was out of chances.

While I wish I could say this diagnosis changed everything for us, it didn't. Sure I worried more, and she made more of an effort to keep her appointments, but she kept scamming. She fell into a "romance scam" where the scammers pretend to be interested in a romantic relationship and they have promised her marriage and a life of love and travel. They used a random white guys photo to catfish her and teach her to add all these secret apps to send money. She has learned so much from them on how to send Ipads in the mail, how to install apps and buy Bitcoin. Some of my anger is that she has learned with them to hurt herself and still cannot understand how to use the Tivo remote control to record her shows. This illness is something I would have to explain to her daily and I am grateful for my medical experience because I was able to be compassionate and patient in how I shared the info.

She became even more attached to the phone. We reported the scammer to Adult Protective Services and The FBI to which they all said to take her phones away. She would just go to Tmobile and buy another phone. She even walked to Target two miles form home one day to get the scammers gift cards and while I was at her house that day wondering where she was, she had fallen in the parking lot and waited at Taco Bell for over an hour to feel better to have enough energy to walk home. She didn't even call us to tell us she had fallen. When she is doing an errand for the scammers she is a different person. The doctors warned us that her brain would change because the toxins that the liver cannot process will go to her brain and her personality will change. She would become so mean and say some of the meanest things I have never thought a mom should say. She has gotten in arguments with literally everyone in her family abroad and here and we have all tried our best.

My dad and sister came to California and stayed a week with her. That was a whole experience as I saw my parents together at dinner again and they were being supportive with each other. My sister who has her own resentment with my mom laid in bed with her several nights as we adjusted her insulin and she was experiencing low insulin in the morning so we needed to monitor the effects. I saw my sister be so patient and loving with her. I witnessed my brother knowing her routine with such discernment. I saw in myself how I would hold my mother's face in my hands and kiss her forehead for maybe the first time ever in my life. I got to be affectionate with her during this long term medical planning. We hired her a caregiver which she quickly had a falling out with when the caregiver tipped us off that my mother had her drive her to the store to buy gift cards again. That was the last argument we had about that scarcity in my mother than was bringing all of us down.

Why am I including all of this as the epigenetic impact of Marianismo? It is a root cause, it is the bloom that a lifetime of being everyone but her truest self. My mom is declining in her health, her memory, and her cognition and yet everyday she reaches for connection through this scam. She even calls it her scammer and insists they love her because they have been with her for one year already. She is dying from this end stage disease and is still in deep scarcity mindset. She is still feeling not enough, not loved enough, not listened to enough, not happy enough, not calm enough. It breaks my heart. It's a weird juxtaposition because I honor her first stance to say, "I have my rights and this is what I choose, I would rather be alone than to give up this part of my life." I see that marianismo has embedded machismo as her first default. She left my dad who managed the finances and schedules for a romance scam where several men pretend to be whomeever she wants them to say they are to successfully obtain all her credit and identity information. The texts messages alone I have cried over at how easily she has told them all of our family information. Most of our family has been impacted from Merida to CA. I may never speak to my uncles and aunt again by the way they have enabled all of this chaos. They visit from Mexico for a week, take her to the bank, the store to get her gift cards, whatever she wants, fights with us because we want her to be protected, and then they leave in a week back to their home, leaving my mother on the outs with her children and in the claws if these scammers.

The outcome of this has been my mom has passed every memory test and advocated for herself in our healthcare meetings. I decided to step away and let her decide her life with her siblings as her spontaneous caregivers. I spent the last three years chasing my mom and really enacting the susto hererado from my lineage and disassociating from my own children who were wanting me. I was tired of fighting everyone to take care of my mom. I was tired of trying to convince her. If she wasn't gravely disabled then I am just running myself ragged. I had to respect her autonomy and mine. Honestly, I miss her so much. I feel in a way, I am not punished with feeling like her, a mom myself raising 3 kids and crying for my mom. I realize I was always a wound for my mom because I am a mirror, a portal for her pain and she would rather live in fantasy where her scarcity vanishes and she is abundant and no longer longing but being. These are the epigenetic impacts of Marianismo in my life and they have very much informed this framework almost as a my grand assignment from ancestors to transmute this pain into collective liberation.

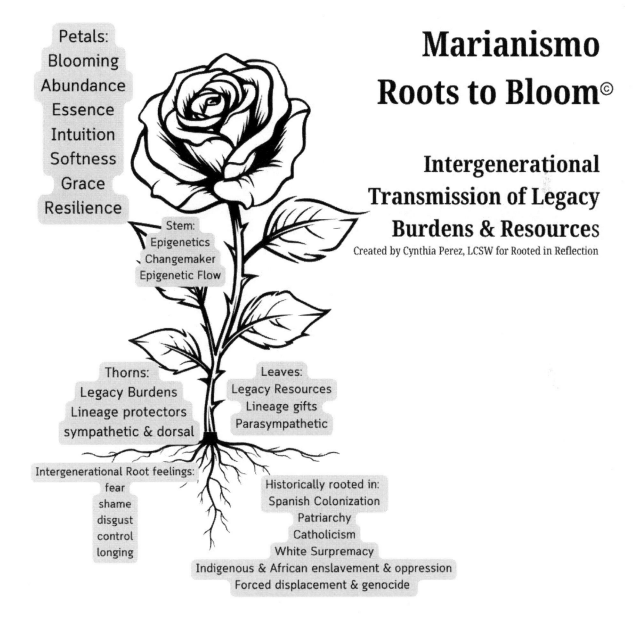

What is "My Marianismo"?

It's naming what root feeling is coming up for me in my body that triggers an impulsive behavior or thought usually rooted in my inherited legacy burdens of marianismo. So I just started calling this root feeling *"My Marianismo"* and became curious to what I could find out about the shadow goodness of Marianismo as a collective with our stories.
So I created spaces called "My Marianismo" for us to unpack what our roots know as a collective.

What are Epigenetic impacts of Marianismo?

"Past research has failed to examine marianismo in relation to multiple cognitive-emotional factors beyond depression, and it remains unclear how the multidimensional construct of marianismo contributes to negative cognitions and emotions in Hispanics."
-NCBI.NLM.nih.gov That is such a limiting statement and we have just accepted that.

We know our bones and chakras hold deep stories of grief and rage which may have led us to not ask about how our pain has led to our illness.

"Epigenetics is the trans generational study of how your behaviors and environment can cause changes that affect the way your genes work." -- cdc.gov
Epigenetics is the study of how the environment and other factors can change the way that genes are expressed. Epigenetics impacts the generation that did not live through the event but carries the DNA of the ancestor with whom embodied their gifts and their trauma. Living in those empowering gifts IS our Epigenetic POWER.

The epigenetic impact of generations of women who were not safe or welcome to be their authentic selves or to create safety for themselves or their families, has had consequences on the body- the physical body, the energy body and the spiritual body. This includes cis-gender heterosexual presenting women, queer womyn,, non binary bodies from puberty to senior years, we have been deeply impacted.

When considering epigenetics and post partum, how do we not also consider how being apart from family, homelands, food or language does not impact a new parent with ancestral attachment wounds? We throw around post partum depression like a curse that has not been cast by colonialism. This is for all the mothers that felt the illness of post partum anxiety due to immigration, mother wounds rooted in abandonment, loss of identity and autonomy rooted in marianismo as a social construct.

Physical illness in Latine/as is of such concern that healthcare centers provide accessible post partum classes and meals for medi-care parents which is lovely. But are we addressing their daily environment and expectations rooted in machismo and colonialism? Are we actually proving care they need or giving ideas of resources before becoming a resource for mother and baby? Are we criminalizing parents seeking asylum with their children without considering the epigentic impact of the intergenerational trauma inflicted with immigration and parent-child separation? When we dehumanize the parents, we harm the children. Our bodies are the keepers or secrets, sadness, and sensory. When we understand our energy around marianismo, we can understand what our bodies have been communicating.

The Duality of Marianismo

"My Marianismo" is me when I am restless and worrying over something I have no control over, but it is also "My Marianismo" that helps me gather community for a collective goal or shows love with a meal and a big hug.

Marianismo represents the duality in womb holders. Though it pressures women to be agreeable and helpful, Marianismo has many facets and emotions that may overrule our own intuition for the believed benefit of the collective rather than the individual (self sacrificing). These responsibilities whether literal or figurative are cultural obligations that create legacy burdens as an expectation for your part in your family's lineage. These legacy burdens are rooted in survival due to oppression and push conforming to social constructs to protect the lineage.

Our harmonious energy, however, shows up when we are able to live in our own legacy resources of our Marianismo. We don't just build families, we can nurture them when we ourselves feel nurtured and tended to. When we show up in our clear intuition and let our chakras glow naturally, we can live in our legacy resources, our natural gifts to the lineage and this actually strengthens our epigenetics for peace, it soothes our nervous system to a parasympathetic state, and it allows us to be in our fullest potential and creative energy.

Colonial Marianismo is the counterpart of Machismo. Machismo has informed, quite literally or symbolically, how a women should show up from how she should dress to how little she should talk. Machismo is a hypermasculine approach to indentifying as a cishet male with a gender caste above a woman and therefore more deserving of the resources and control in the family.

Marianismo also informs machismo as the wombholder creates life and opens up the portal of marianismo roots; healed or unhealed. The colonized indigenous "mother wound" of marianismo raises the belief around gender and status. This is why marianismo as a legacy resource is intergenerational healing. Historically, mothers are the spiritual pillars of the family. Patriarchy has kept marianismo expectations humble, scrutinized and rigorous. Understanding marianismo is the home and the imprint for gender norms as burdens or sourced love, we have capacity to make a huge paradigm shifts. We can expand our idea of gender expectations as a barrier to our connection to our children and ourselves.

The Decolonized Marianista acknowledges the burdens of the land, the lineage and the legacy they have inherited while also conjuring up the wisdom, intuition and life force energy of their own divine legacy resources through ancestral connection, prana energy sourcing and epigenetic flow from a parasympathetic state.

Machismo as the counterpart

The construct of machismo describes beliefs and expectations regarding the role of men in society; it is a set of values, attitudes, and beliefs about masculinity, or what it is to be a man. Machismo encompasses positive and negative aspects of masculinity, including bravery, honor, dominance, aggression, sexism, sexual prowess, and reserved emotions, among others Machismo also includes deep rooted beliefs that consider it appropriate for women to remain in traditional roles, this encourages male dominance over women.
.
When I ask about patriarchy in group spaces, most people, including men, have a physical reaction to the word "Macho" or "Machismo". Surprisingly and optimistically, even men have stood up in spaces and shared how machismo has made them unsafe as a child and an adult. This paradigm is not one of bringing family together but of controlling family using the colonizer's tools of religious dogma, gender standards, and shame as a tool of creating a traumatized people who will oblige and teach others to submit to the dogma for safety.

Machismo is gendered but also rooted in white supremacy and proximity to whiteness. As a colonized people we were taught through conquest by castes that proximity to whiteness means safety and more advancement. It may even be unconscious. Internalized racism can lead women to want to marry a partner with proximity to whiteness and women put up with it because of what they feel they will gain from it or the attractiveness of priviledge.

Other examples of legacy burdens women inherit due to patriarchy
"Strong Black Woman"- Resilient, tireless, strong, creative, usually with little consideration of the cost to her wellness to be all the roles.
"Mammy"- caricature during Jim Crow Era that showed Black enslaved women as happy, content and loyal as a way to show enslavement had "humanity"

Tiger Mom, a very strict mother who makes her child work very hard at school, and at other activities such as music, in order to be successful This phrase was first used to describe the strict style of bringing up children thought to be typical of parents in China and East Asia.

Understanding the emotional roller coaster of Marianismo means also understanding and feeling the energy of Machismo.

What is Machismo and what how did it play a role in my childhood?
What does machismo sound like?
What does Machismo feel like?
How does my body feel when I think about machismo?

My Marianismo- What's Mine and what's coming up

The term has been around for over 50 years, that word. But my marianismo, when I say **my marianismo**, is really just owning it, claiming it.

Instead of shaming what comes up for me when I'm feeling left out or jealous or scared, if I claim it as, **that's my marianismo showing up**, my shadow self, my mother wounds and my mother's protective intentions. Naming it has allowed me to give it a face, to give it an experience and not just shame it. So when I say that's "my marianismo", it's my way of really labeling the legacy burdens within me.

Just calling this root feeling **my marianismo**, it's allowing me to be curious as to, **where does this come from? What is the root of this?**

In 2021 I did not see spaces talking about this mother wound rooted in historical trauma, so I created spaces. I haven a six- week groups. I have CEU courses. I have one -to -one coaching on really just unpacking what is my marianismo? What is your marianismo? What does it look like?

What kind of marianismo was passed down to me as modeled by the mother that I had or the tias that raised me or my grandmother? Where, or better yet, how deep does this marianismo go? Really just honoring what is within us and also what we might want to tease out as our resources.

This conversation is really about the duality of marianismo.

The duality of marianismo because we want to acknowledge that marianismo is not just when we are not being in our highest self, when we are rageful or jealous, yes that can be marianismo acting from a place of fear or scarcity but there's also duality in marianismo and I want to highlight that.

When I'm feeling like I don't know what to do. I'm stuck. I feel like I made a mistake and I don't know how to get back on track and maybe feelings of guilt, shame, judgment come up. I want you to think about the duality of it.
How am I in my resource and how am I in my legacy burdens? So Marianismo has the duality. It is me when I'm restless and I'm worrying that over something that I really can't control.
But it's also "my marianismo" when I shake it off, maybe I dance, I make a really good meal, and then I go outside for a walk and I'm able to chat with my neighbors in a really embodied way. It's both, do you see? It's the resource that I'm able to pull out my magic, but it's also the epigenetic trauma of my people.

The Roots

"No tengo dinero para darte pero si tengo un corazón y unas manos para ayudarte."
— mi Abuela Raquel

"What is your home and do you feel a connection? If our homes have been vandalized, removed; if we have been kidnapped and sold like cattle from a Home; if we have witnessed extreme poverty despite excessive labor while Home, then can we feel **safe**? Will this lack of safety not produce a set of symptoms?" Mullan, J 2023 *Decolonizing Therapy Oppression, Historical Trauma and Politicizing Your Practice*

The Roots are beyond what we can see as our home and are felt throughout the home. The roots are the past histories we may or may not have access to. The knowing of our roots and connection to where our people come from is in it of itself a privilege.

This book is a way of seeing marianismo and explaining it in a way that not only made sense to my way of learning, but in my spirit. It addressed the areas I found were lacking in other discussions in mental health. It feels like I have always meant to create this and I am barely catching up with my roots. The roots of my research started in between infertility complications by miscarriage and throughout my post partum fog. I was working as a medical social worker for 5 years at this time and I had been working with mostly geriatrics and people with chronic pain and comorbidity with complex symptoms. I was a home health social worker and would visit people in their homes. I saw many clients with diabetes for various issues and I learned so much about diabetes care from that job and yet I had never considered the root cause. I started to wonder why so many patients had uncontrolled diabetes and learned depression and diabetes were linked. I took CE courses to learn more about diabetes and mental health. That led me into a rabbit hole of info that just tickles my neuroexpanisve brain and I delight in getting to the root of things. I started researching how diabetes could be managed by a healthy environment where the body feels safety. I read how toxic stress has a major impact on diabetes and the body's organs over time. I also became fascinated in post partum depression among mothers. I read an article that stated Latina mothers in the US reported 52% post partum depression compared to Non Latina US Mothers reporting 15% with post partum depression (Lara-Cinisomo, Sandraluz, et al.,).

My first thought after reading that article was, "I bet it's higher in Latinas because they didn't disclose or they weren't assessed". My own post partum shadows revealing themselves with interest in getting to the bottom of these deep relentless feelings of fear and grief I had unlocked with me since giving birth. I had this knowing that I was not the only one. I heard my thoughts and my conscience followed, "you're a medical social worker, what are you going to do about it?". That led me down a rabbit hole to land back in my Xicana passion for talking about marianismo. The roots of this "theory" I will present in the following pages are my own ideas and connections except when referenced and cited. The roots of this body of work is rooted in my own soul dismemberments in 2016, 2020, and again in 2024, each time rebirthing a stronger Spirit in me than the woman I was before. This book is also asking to be written. Much of these roots are my ancestors guiding me and me finally trusting us all enough to listen and follow through with what stirs up in me as mine. The roots of our illness or "behaviors" or "symptoms" or "sadness" is the similar for us in the collective Latino African Caribbean Filipino Diaspora and it's one of colonial and religious trauma that we have mistaken as ours to uphold. The roots want to tell their story.

My Marianismo
Epigenetic impact on The Roots

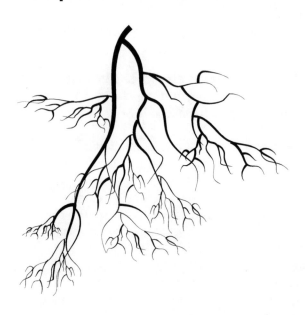

The epigenetics of historical trauma is passed through the roots through 7 generations on each side. Marianismo is a cultural value created out of survival & assimilation of those displaced into the diasporas colonized by Spain & forced into Catholicsm is passed through the roots as information for survival of colonialism, displacement, ancestral attachment trauma, genocide of indigenous & African lineages. The roots send messages as information on the environment based on past survival.

Root feelings
fear, shame, rage, disgust, control, grief, longing, scarcity

Feelings can look like
overextending, shrinking, humility, distrust, disconnected, restless, enraged, numb

Historical Trauma can remember abandon, separation, violence, abuse, genocide, lack, ancestral attachment trauma, colonization

This impacts the root and solar plexus charkas.

The Roots

I'm a very visual person. I need to be able to see it. I hope to create a visual of historical roots of marianismo using some of my own stories and some original frameworks and theories tying it together with our mental health and nervous system. I invite you to consider any small roots to bloom moments you've had and feel free to claim it, to not minimize the impact and life path it has created. Take up the space and time to include yourself in caring for everyone.

Thinking about when you see a beautiful red rose, or a purple rose, or a fragrant white rose, thinking about how good it smells, how it attracts you, how it calls you. Historically roses are used on altars as protection. Roses are used in teas, baths, and as gifts.

The Virgin Mary appeared to Juan Diego, an Aztec convert to Christianity, in 1531, and this event is known as the Apparitions of Our Lady of Guadalupe. Roses are also what was found on the lining of the cloak of La Virgen de Guadalupe, the legend told to the indigenous people to submit us to Catholicism. Roses were on the cloak of the Virgin Mary, again, talking about protection, but also this is an indigenous plant that has been used for love, softness, and protection. It's very symbolic and resilient. So let's just think about how we are a rose, this beautiful rosebud that is us and our experience and how we show up.

But what is beneath that rose? Can we think of the roots in the terms of intergenerational, so crossing generations from one to the next to the next, intergenerational transmission, crossing generations of legacy burdens. Things that we've had to carry in our lineage. These burdens may be as obvious as the neighborhood you live in and the access to safety in your home and as nuanced as invisible gender rules that dictate how a young lady or womb holder is supposed to behave in her family to honor God and aspire to be as humble as the Virgin Mary.

The beauty of roots is the depth of resilience for survival. We have resources that made future generations possible.

Whether we know them or not, subconscious or conscious, we all have legacy resources, things that we have inherited that are helpful or good for us, we carry within us.

At the root of who we are or the behavior lies many stories woven together like roots spreading throughout the soil, expanding and rooting where they spread. So looking at the roots of marianismo, we start at the roots of our colonized peoples and the lands and the impact of the historical trauma of colonization, capitalism, encomienda, gender and racial castes, and the genocide of indigenous people and traditions by the Spanish Catholic Church and what would become The United States, Mexico, Puerto Rico, Latin America and the diasporas and the Phillipines.

This book is specific and also relatable for many cultures and generations. Many islands and I

The Roots of Marianismo

lands were colonized by Spain and indoctorinated in Catholicsm. The Americas, Africa, and the Phillipines were colonized and indoctorinated by Spain. The stress of the eldest Filipina daughter to be obedient and successful may look similar to a Mexican way of being a "good daughter". Spain brought enslaved peoples from parts of Africa they colonized and they were forced into a caste system that made enslavement and indentured servitude part of the colonized economy. Africans and Indigenous peoples of the Americas and islands created new lineages of Afro-Mestizos or Afro-Indigenous or Mestizos. Tulane university mentions the historical legacy resources of Africans history and the collaboration of both cultures."African influences are seen and felt in Brazil from Candomblé to Capoeira; in Cuba through Santeria and Salsa; and in Peruvian music and their Pacific coast communities. The African presence extends through Colombia, Ecuador, Panama, Venezuela, and throughout Latin America" Afro-Mexicans: Illuminating the invisible from past to present.

Starting at the roots, we see that marianismo, the term, the value, the behavior, the role is rooted in, and this is what makes it so specific and, you know, feelable, but it's rooted in Spanish colonization. So maybe your Filipino friend can relate to this, this is part of the Diaspora of people colonized by Spain.

So it's specifically rooted in Spanish colonization. It's rooted in patriarchy. The men are to serve God and the women is to serve the man. She's there to chase the man, to make sure he's fed, he's safe. The children are tended to. It is specifically really patriarchy led, centered. And this is how they created machismo and marianismo, this partnership of service to God.

This is like a skewed version of a hyper elevated version of patriarchy, machismo and marianismo. So it's rooted in this, which is very limiting, right? And can often have violence or fear. It's rooted in Catholicism.

If you've grown up in Catholicism and you have positive experiences, that's great. And also equally important is what has happened historically to Indigenous communities that had to either die, be separated from their family, or be separated from their own spirit, their true self, in the name of Catholicism.

Marianismo root healing challenges us to look at how Catholicism has taken so many Indigenous practices and intertwined them into Catholicism. The smoke, the plantitas, right, the four directions, the way that we do certain traditions, the skewing of it, taking, borrowing, renaming, restoring. And now we are kind of confused about what is ours, but also with the indoctorination of Catholicism, shaming, labeling, anything other than worshiping Jesus. So if we're doing meditation or we wanna do oracle or tarot cards, we wanna go see a shaman, we wanna do an ayahuasca, we feel, my gosh, I am gonna be such a bad person because I wanna try plant medicine. This is this epigenetic root, rooted in Catholicism and very much,

The Inquisition, the encomienda, genocide of if you're not Catholic, you could very well have been killed seven generations ago. So it's rooted in this commitment to Catholicism. So it's gonna show up, it's gonna show up.

White supremacy is very much noted as the Spanish had a caste system. The Spanish upheld slavery. Not only did they bring enslaved Africans from different parts of Africa or the Caribbean or the islands over on their ships, they created a caste system of who was deemed "worthy" in a hierachy ladder of socialization and safety. At the top were the white Europeans, the Spanish. And even within the Spanish, there were different castes. Peninsulares were considered most noble, Criollos, and then Mestizos, with skin color dictating the measure of status even in this level. The bottom was indigenous and Black persons. Many histories tell how indigenous and Africans worked together in uprising and in celebration (music, food, lineages) as a way of preserving the culture and creating collective safety. This is juxtaposed with others who, as colonialism strives, denounced any indigineity or African roots to maintain their social status.

Something that has been ingrained since that colonial violence and it has been really see the roots are in the mud it's been muddied it's been intertangled in now how our root belief system goes and it's not right it is colonization that's all we think it's like the right way to do things but it's actually oppression.

The Roots of Colonial Marianismo expectations

Rooted in abandonment attachment, wounds due to immigration, vulnerability in relationships is difficult. It feels unsafe to be vulnerable. It might be taken from you. It might be squandered. It might be held against you to be vulnerable. Okay, so those are legacy burdens of marianismo. So I might be cold or not share.

The impulse to shrink. Think about how many ancestors had to swallow their words or feelings and shrink. Imagine the body constantly turning on the switch the get as small as possible?

"When is comes to experiences of racism and oppression, even when you receive love and support you can still develop PTSD or CPTSD, because feeling othered every day can rob you of your sense of safety in the world."
— Natalie Y. Gutiérrez LMFT, The Pain We Carry: Healing from Complex PTSD for People of Color

This one's really big. This impulse to have to be humble, to have to close up, to have to hide and not be seen. Consider that this legacy burden has been passed down to you through your abuelos, abuelas, your mother, your dad, your caregivers, to just disappear, to not be seen. Because think about it, maybe in our parents' generation, maybe it meant they would get in trouble with their parents, they would get beat, they would get punished.

But maybe for their parents, your grandparents or your great grandparents, it literally meant life or death to be seen, to show up, to not be humbled, to be braggadocious. It could have meant death. So we have learned how to disappear, how to be humble, and it is in our DNA. And so think about that now when we're trying to show up as our authentic self and it feels hard and it feels like we're cased in. We have like a casting around our nervous system that shudders with a "No, shrink, staying this small is safest". And it almost like poofs us back. And really just trying to see, my gosh, how has humility kept my people safe in the past? But also how is it keeping me small now? And how do I need to shake it off because it's no longer serving me?

So the impulse to shrink or perform for safety is neuro biological in the energy body, our physical energy body. Okay. And there is fear of never being enough or never having enough. So this makes us have to perform or chase or do or juggle. And we're always going to be searching for that approval or that, wow, that celebration in others. And really it's telling us that we're connected and we're safe.

And these are burdens because it tends to be taken advantage of. We tend to over perform or over deliver or be all for our productivity and consider if that is actually doing us harm. And some of the legacy resources, let's get into that. Let's shift gears into some legacy resources. Okay. Now, if you heard the burdens and you're like, gosh, yes, yes, I know someone that has all of that. Let's look into the legacy resources and maybe.

They're not calling them that maybe you're not calling them that and we can actually Practice what we talked about in burdens of being humble.
How could you embody these resources of marianismo? Now these are just a few. I totally invite you to write your own list. Not even just a list of what your legacy resources are, but what other people who you admire, what are their legacy resources?

Can you imagine what it would feel like in a liberated decolonized energy and physical body? Wow. Can you imagine the energy you will attract? Let's imagine it here.
Feel free to draw in resources and symbolism of your liberated spirit and body.

My liberated decolonized body

Divine Timing in Divine Time

From 2021-2024 I created continuing education courses for therapists and providers on the impact of marianismo. I have spoken about the topic on my podcast and in group workshops with such passion that at times I myself wondered, why do I care so much when I am part of the Spanish colonization in my genes as much as I am indigenous to Yucatan? In divine timing and ancestral guidance, it was 2024 in working with Irisneri Alicea Flores, owner of Descubre Tu Historia and Boriqua geneaologist, put a piece of my personal marianismo puzzle together. She reported that yes, my maternal grandfather Mario did migrate to Ventura County to become a farm worker and gain residency for his family. He did marry in Merida, Yucatan where he would raise 7 children with his wife, Elide.

She also showed me birth and death certificates as far back as my great great great grandparents whom were born in Mani, Yucatan. I remember visiting Mani when I was 25 and my tio suggested I go eat at his father's favorite restaurant, "El Principe de Mani". I tell this story in my recorded webinar. I made it to that restaurant by miracle, or maybe by my ancestors. I came to discover the history of Spanish colonization specifically at Mani. It was the site of the encomiendas. It was at Mani where the Spanish burned the maya codices and stole gold and tools while forcing the indigenous maya to choose the fate of indoctorination of Catholicism or death. It made sense that day that I as both colonizer and colonized have a duty to talk about this history and the impact we are living out now as we falsely call it our "personality" our our "culture".

The first Spanish church in Yucatan built at Mani. This was the site of "Baptisms" and religious reform of indigenous Yucatec Maya people

My maternal grandparents in their home in Merida. My grandfather from Mani, Yucatan.

My great grandmother Aurora "Lola" born in Mani, Yucatan, Mx

El Principe de Mani restaurant. Delicious traditional Yucatec cuisine. A family recommended stop.

History OF MANI, YUCATAN
"What is the history of Maní Magical Town?
"The history of Maní dates back to the pre-Hispanic era when it was an important ceremonial and commercial center for the ancient Maya civilization. During this time, it was ruled by the cacicazgo (chiefdom) of Maní de Tutul Xiú and served as a ceremonial site where offerings were made for the annual festival honoring Kukulcán." -pueblosmagicostrenmaya .com.

"Fray Diego de Landa established an Inquisition tribunal in Maní, Yucatán. He conducted the 'Act of Faith', during which a considerable number of sacred images, objects, and Maya codices were incinerated as part of the Franciscan movement to convert the indigenous people to Christianity." - pueblosmagicostrenmaya.com

The pueblo of Mani, now called, El Pueblo Magico was an important ceremonial and commercial center for the ancient Maya civilization. During this time, it was ruled by the chiefdom of Mani, the Tutul Shu, and served as a ceremonial site where offerings were made for the annual festival honoring Kukulkan, the god of wind, rain, and storms.

But the other part, that's the first history, the first known indigenous history of Mani, the site of Mayas. That must not be understated or glossed over.

But then there's the second part, the colonized part of Mani. Frey Diego de Landa established an inquisition tribunal in Mani, Yucatan. He conducted the Act of Faith during which a considerable number of sacred images, objects, and Maya codices were incinerated as part of the Franciscan movement to convert the indigenous people to Christianity. When I read that last part, I still have emotion when I read it. It's like my Yucatec Maya body knows. Right now it feels like grief, but I really believe that when I was discovering all this in my own body, it felt like rage. And as I go deeper, I realized this is not just mine, but it's my ancestors pushing me to find all this out about us.

I met with a genealogist, a genealogist, Irisneri of Descubre tu Historia. She is from Puerto Rico, and not only is she ancestrally protected in this calling she has, she's really helpful because she can read the old school documents in Spanish. Thankfully, she found that my family all the way from the 1600s and remember in the 1500s the Spanish arrived and they just burnt so much of the lineage. So really this information is showing that my lineage started in Mani, Yucatan, the southern most tip of Mexico.

I saw six generations up of ancestors from this small pueblo in Mani. And the sad thing is, is this is the church they built. The first church, if you think about it, Yucatan is a peninsula. So this was the first port of entry. And it's deep in this pueblo, this jungle town. And they would gather the indigenous people there. And you either chose to get baptized Catholic and pofess your commitment to the church at this site or you were killed.
That very much happened to Yucatec Maya lineage. I feel it every time I talk about it. So a funny, not a funny story, but like a beautiful story that keeps giving to me as I do this work. If you Google Mani, what may pop up is restaurant named El Principe de Mani. That's what it's called. I've gone back to Yucatan, like what I see now is like ceremonial times that I felt called to go.

I have returned to Merida, Yucatan at really pivotal moments, five, 10, 15, 20, 25. And at 20, I went and I remember I was with friends and I was so excited for them to see where my family grew up. One trip my uncle said, you should go visit Mani and go eat at this place called El Principe de Mani. And he told me what to order. He told me it was delicious that I wouldn't be disappointed. So me and my friends, we rented a car, blasted the AC and headed out to explore.

We had gone to see Chichen Itza and we were on our way back and I insisted we stop at the town of Mani. I didn't know that that's where my family was from. I probably heard my uncle tell me but didn't really care because I'm like, *what does it have to do with me?* Right? I'm 20. And I kid you not, we were driving through the town and I'm realizing, this is un pueblo. There were not stops signs or corporate shops. There were malnourished dogs on most corners and homes made of mud, tin, wood and palm fronds. This is what they meant and I felt instantly, cosmically connected while also never having been anywhere like this place before.

Truth be told, before arriving to Mani from el castillo at Chichen Itza, we had to pull over throughout the route into the pueblos several times and ask people that were coming outside of their homes or laying in their hamacas outside. We were like, "excuse me, we're looking for a principe". The instructions were, "go down three trees and to the, after three trees, there's going to be a dog laying on the corner. Then when you see the dog, make a right, then you're going to see an old lady's house. It's pink, make a left." You know, it was these very, small town instructions and I thought, oh my gosh how will we ever find it? This was before Google, before we could do driving directions but thanks to the people and ancestors, we found it.

I'm not kidding you, when I ate the pok chuk that my uncle recommended I felt emotional. I know it was a spiritual moment because my friends ate their food like it was another day, another meal. But I was warmed up inside. He also recommended that I get a "Chela" which is a frosted glass with beer with lemon and salt. It was a hot and humid day And I just remember when I had that meal, I felt at home. Not even fully allowing myself to be received and loved on by the land, the food alone nurtured me in a way I still feel in my cellular memory. I felt my grandfathers drinking the icy cold beer and sighing through me, "todo bien, todo bien".
I thought, and this is like 20 years ago, cause I'm 40 now, I thought then, well it's because I'm really happy that I found this place. I thought this is my ego.

That's why it feels so good. And now 20 years later, I realized, okay, same place, solar plexus, but it's not my ego. It was actually connection to myself, connection to my body, connection to my epigenetic, connection to my ancestors. But I didn't call it that then. I didn't even consider that maybe the land was calling me back.

Maybe the food wanted me to taste it, maybe Mani was calling me. Because I can still remember where I was at that restaurant and I can still remember the drive and it still means so much. Just a few months ago, as I'm talking to Irisneri, the genealogist, shares that my maternal grandfather Mario was born and raised in Mani.

He came to California as a small boy to escape his abusive stepfather. That is how we got our lineage in California. But make no mistakes, before Merida, he was a small boy in Mani. My grandmother seen here, this is her pic from her U.S. immigration papers in 1961. When I read her citizenship papers, she was quoted saying, "I've never left My small town of Mani. This is My first time arriving to California" and she was in her 60s.

And I say all this to say that I have sat on this book and my virtual courses because I felt like, who am I to talk about this? I'm an American with this lineage, but like I didn't grow up there. I'm not from there. And you know, I have this guilt for my white skin. I have this shame for my light eyes. I feel, you know, decades of this duality in my genes, right?

I have the genes of the colonizer and the colonized.
And my land says it. Where I come from is a historic place of conflict for my people. And that makes up me. And in reading this and really holding space and allowing myself to be thankful to my ancestors for showing me this, I take this and I take it very seriously.
When I think this is my Marianismo journey, I wonder how many of us are living our lives without really acknowledging how important it is that we're here. Because as I started to study more, I learned that the Spanish killed 85 to 90 % of My population, whether through infection, illnesses, or genocide.

I'm here. I'm here because of my ancestors and because of their Marianismo.
And now, I truly believe that what they want most for me is to unburden myself because they know the burden of a life of Marianismo.
They want to share the gifts of Marianismo. And they want me to forget the having to shrink because they realize that I'm safe now. And so when we think about Marianismo really inviting ourselves, this is an invitation, this space, right? And this intention that you pour in just being here on your own.

It's an acknowledgement. I say this all with a deep breath and con todo cariño because we're all kind of unraveling these deep roots and knowing that it's not your fault, this deep history of colonization and yet what you choose to carry moving forward after you know this awareness.

When I think about my roots I also think about our cosmology. As below with rose roots we see the past, we can considered our cosmology the magic above that led us to our current destinies.
The US Department of Energy states 'cosmology studies how the history of the universe led to the stars, galaxies, and other features we can observe today. Cosmology is the study of the origin, development, structure, history, and future of the entire universe." www.energy.gov

When thinking of how the Mayas saw cosmology they referenced the stars, moon, sun and cycles. They considered it more than intellectual research, they saw it as a soul lesson. Turning towards our cosmology leads us on a personal spiritual quest, a journey of self-discovery and awakening to the mysteries of our existence and past cycles. "In their reverence for the natural world, their understanding of time as cyclical, and their recognition of the interconnectedness of all things, we find echoes of timeless truths that resonate with the deepest reaches of our souls." sacredearthjourneys.ca/blog/exploring-maya-cosmology/

My Mother's Roots

When my mom was ten years old she immigrated from Yucatan with her father, paternal grandmother Lola, and her five siblings. They traveled in a station wagon for 10 days until they reached Oxnard, CA to see the home their parents had worked the last two years to purchase for them as a family. Finally reunited, my mom started 5th grade in English at an Oxnard Elementary and loved it! She felt special. When school was out on vacation she worked in the fields picking fruit as well as being trained in the canneries sorting vegetables with her mother. She said she enjoyed it. She was happy to be learning English. She said her dad would always move her throughout her life back and forth to Mexico through the seasons of the fieldwork but also through the seasons of her feminine development. When she was a teenager her dad would control every interaction she had with boys. This would set the foundation of my mother's nervous system and attachment. This would also activate the ancestral attachment wound in her lineage.

In her 20's my mom worked at the Merida airport in her homeland of Yucatan, Mexico announcing the flights on the intercom.My dad always said he loved hearing her voice over the radio and tells the story of sounding like she was working on the mic when reciting her vows. My parents were married at 25 years old, they had my sister in Yucatan and then moved to California to start a new life. Since her parents were field workers, the family had residency in the United States and my father wanted to raise his family in California, by the beach, like home on Progreso Beach.

My mom was a trained typist, bilingual, and eager to work a teacher's schedule so she could vacation in Yucatan in the summer. Luckily she was hired as a secretary to work at an elementary school because of her "fast hands.

I think about how my mom has made a living with her "fast hands" her whole life. From picking defective peppers off a conveyor belt to stacking luggage and dictating flights, my mom has been a multitasker all her life. Now they call it "bi-lateral stimulation" but when she was an immigrant it was called survival. As a secretary she was the only non American person working in the office in 1984 at a high school in Torrance, a city in the county of Los Angeles.
I remember one day she cried because they scolded her for taking a personal call from my dad and speaking to him in Spanish because no one else could understand her. She was written up and told she was not allowed to speak Spanish at work unless it is for school personnel. As if that didn't make her feel excluded enough, they placed her desk in a corner so her face was not facing the front of the office like the others she shared an office with. When she told me this, I felt sacred rage in my body, and I also felt the energy of how demoralizing that felt and the impact it had on her nervous system, daily. From the fields to the schools, she was using her gifts of fast hands and fast dictation for production, not creation. There are so many nuances in this page that we minimize and accept as "no big deal". It is a great big deal how we do all of this in the eco-systems we were raised in. With no end in sight, it becomes who we are.
 My legacy is our legacy.

It came to me in a meditation one day, the gratitude for the synchronicity that I am doing that now, too-but for my own bloom. I get to be creative and she dictated for others. I have a podcast and get to speak on a mic and preserve our stories and language is an important part of my work. Naming this legacy work we do, naming the historical trauma we feel in our bones. I have self published journals I dictate to myself and type out with my s l o w h a n d s. I get to be creative and have my mom's magic to support my work now. It's a beautiful awareness. I allow myself to expand for myself and my lineage.

Noticing Marianismo in the home

"Three generations--the expectant parent, the fetus, and the eggs in that fetus's ovaries--can be genetically altered by stressors during pregnancy. By understanding this, you can see that both cultural and family legacy burdens are not just beliefs; they're also physically expressed."
— Natalie Y. Gutiérrez LMFT, <u>The Pain We Carry: Healing from Complex PTSD for People of Color</u>

What did Marianismo look like in my childhood home?

What was my mother's childhood like with machismo?

How was my relationship with my mother strained by machismo?

What does My Marianismo look like?

My Marianismo and the Inner Child Wound

Just the header on this page has my inner child feeling some kind of way about how I talk about my own mother or how I honor thy mother in this book. That is my inner child feeling the need to dismiss parts of her story (once again) to honor her elder's. This is not just an epigenetic pull to keep secrets and keep appearances, this is also my inner child fear of disappointing my own mother. My own wounds come long before I was even born. My wounds have cellular fragments from my great grandparents and still inform the dance my mother and I do now. Let me explain.

In Season 3 Episode 4 of Confetti All Around Podcast, I host a solo episode entitled, "La Llorona: Not Dead but Not Alive Either" where I share some of my post partum experience of what I called "being in the fog". I felt not dead, but not alive, always longing for a quiet place away from my own internal thoughts and fears. I explain the epigenetics of panic and worry in my lineage as the story of my grandfather Mario leaving his mother at the age of 11 to travel to the United States in search of a better life and away from his abusive stepfather. My great grandmother Aurora missed her son, my grandfather, so much that every day that he was gone she would cry on the beach of Chicxulub and search for him at the pier of Progreso Beach, Yucatan in hopes that her son had returned.

My grandfather left his land from the ages of 11-14 to escape his abusive step father and to see what he could find for himself. This led to my great grandmother Lola longing to make this loss right. Lola had also lost 2 of her own very young children prior to that. So when her oldest son left in protest of his step father, well that right there changed the next part of their lives and they didn't even know it yet.
Worried she would never see her son Mario again, when he returned home after 3 years of traveling throughout the U.S. on a labor ship, she committed to always help him care for himself and his family. This root fear of abandonment and child loss would haunt me through my stem as a new mother. This longing and yearning for home and safety would awaken as post partum grief.

The way my great grandmother Lola (her nickname) stayed true to her word would be her lifelong offering of herself to help Mario raise his children. Lola would go on to watch my mom and her 6 siblings while her parents traveled back and forth from Yucatan to Oxnard, CA six months out of the year to pick fruit, work at the canneries and climb the American economic ladder. But back at home, Lola had more than a handful. She was in charge of 6 grandchildren whom missed their own parents and did not have the space to know who they are with their parents home with them on the daily. I believe this history of intergenerational longing, worry, wonder, disassociation, rejection, humility, and distrust was the threading of my own inner epigenetic body.

When I think about the inner child in Marianismo expectations I see her/them trying to be all the things. If I am being detailed and honest, I see my inner child about 7 years old, wearing a pearl necklace, a black and white polka dot dress to her knees, grown woman heels that are obviously too big. I see her hair pinned up with a couple curls at the bangs, she is holding a big boxy purse and wondering how to apply the red lipstick in her hand. She loves that it is bright red and how beautiful her own mother looks all dolled up. She knows what she SHOULD DO, she just never expected all the feelings to follow. My inner child is who I task to carry out my Marianismo burdens. Don't get me wrong, she does it, sometimes, she delights in it. She used to love getting to pretend to be the mom anyway so this should be a piece of flan!, Easy peasey. Except it is overwhelming and lonely.

My Marianismo and the Inner Child Wound

The thing is my inner child has her own experience with motherhood. One is a lived experience that she woke up to everyday and felt in her spunky chubby body. The other one is the motherhood experience she feels through her own mother's lived childhood, her grandmother's motherhood, and her great grandmother's maternal traumas and reconciliations. Whew, read that back because that's a lot! Took me years post partum to untangle this ball of yarn and find my own body at the center.

When I am activated by my maternal worry or fear, not only am I responding to the present reality, but if I am in sympathetic mode, I am tapping into my epignetic reserves so to speak and unlocking some past survival codes to push through unbearable or unknown feelings. When I need to cope with my motherhood, my own epigenetics guides my unconscious inner mother.

But what about that inner child? Who guides her, if not me?

Ah, that is where I have found my compass getting me lost. My inner child is guided by my own real experiences of my mother sprinkled with my co-dependent wishes for her to finally choose me. Truth finds it hard to tell my inner child that she has always been enough and also sadly, my mother has been parenting me from her inner child wounds that always longed for her mother whom was always in another place than she was. Sorry mija, that's the truth of it. That's the naranja agria you come from.

"Anywhere but here, anyone but you" I started to label this feeling of "never enoughness" I felt projected on me from my mother. The thing is my mom always longed for her mom, and her mom longed for her mom, and here I was longing for my own mother to see me, feel my warmth, and she couldn't. Her inner child was sitting in her adult body ready to be picked up from her maternal responsibilities and held by her own mother and dismissed from this other life of being constantly wanted instead of constantly cared for. It cost *little me* so much time and pain everyday when she didn't even notice the love she did have. The love I offered in various actions. I would sing to my mom, first for my own pleasure of singing, but secondly to maybe snap her out of her sad trance of wishing she was with "them". "Her Family". And *little me* would turn the singing into humming and the humming would turn to crying because who was I if not too, "her family"? I never saw it until I became a mom, the two of us, sitting in our own rooms crying for our mothers to hold us, hers in Mexico and mine in the next room watching novelas, and neither of us feeling held.

I notice this now as I confront my own marianismo inner child wound. I with my own children saw that I was down right shocked at how hard it is to be a parent but also once I was in this portal, I expected more tools, more guides, more whimsical landscapes. This was no picnic in the woods! This was the trenches!!

My inner child, if not comforted and reassured, can fall into the socialized trap of putting everyone before her. It is from the same recipe for children and women to historically consider others before their own autonomy, interests and happiness. My role now is to always be a loving inner guide for all ages she shows up as and work from a loving lens at knowing the parts of us we used to reject as parts of our team. We get to be the mother we needed and hoped for, to ourselves everyday with re-parenting our mother wounds.

My Marianismo and the Inner Child Wound

This is where we can do the inner child work to remind ourselves that we are not waiting to be loved, we are love, we create it within us despite what we were given and we can ask the child within us, "how have you longed to be mothered?" and if they open up can we intuitively ask, "May I re-mother you in the times that feel foggy?".

Remind her/them that they are as still deserving of the parent they longed for and the adult they hoped to become.

They can be their own parent, a pretty damn good one, at that.
It reminds me of when I became a step parent to my son at age 26years old. I had never had step parents and had no clue how to support him but to respect his process. I remember the advice I would give him after he endured family drama of his own, "Honey, you have 4 families and while it is great when it comes to birthdays, it is also a lot of people showing up how they show up. Observe it. notice it but don't take it all in. Keep the good you see in your family, even me, and keep those gems. The other parts you see in us that are protective, our unhealed controlling parts, leave those parts and learn from us. Grow the good." That's what my inner teenager told my stepson when he/we didn't know how else to make this deep entangled pain make sense. I hope that makes sense.

An invitation into YOUR Marianismo

Okay so, con todo cariño, I promise this is all written with your golden light energy as the intention.

This is an invitation to bring out your light force energy at all its power and not just acknowledge it.... cozy up to it, clear it, step into its warmth and clarity.
When considering your energy field due to Marianismo root beliefs, this is an invitation to lovingly observe yourself and bring yourself to the front to create the ceremony or initiation of your lived purpose as you live in your legacy resources.

Can you reflect on the energy of your Marianismo protectors as a burden? What would you like to let go of? Imagine your pain like dropping sandbags off the side of your hot air balloon, what heavy burdens would you get rid of?

What parts of your marianismo are strong and nurturing?

What ways of being do you want to protect and strengthen?

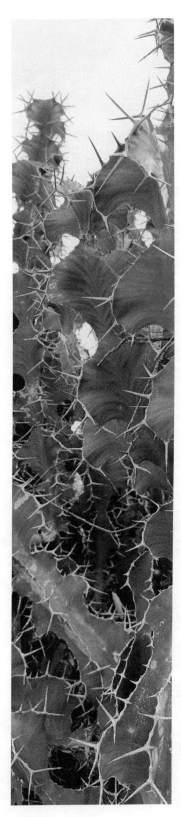

MY MOM'S SCARS ARE MY SACRED GRIEF

"The day you finally start dealing with your past is the day you stop dragging it into the present."
Diane Guerrero, In the Country We Love: My Family Divided

WHAT IS MY SACRED RAGE & GRIEF?

"Rage is the love child of ancestral trauma and shame" says the Rage Doctor herself, Dr. Jennifer Mullan of Decolonizing Therapy. When we really sit with this and digest what we have been carrying we can get a wider view on what stories are being told to us through this sacred rage?

Have you been dismissed or ostracized for your anger or grief? Maybe you have been told by your family to just "be grateful".

Our **ancestral attachment trauma**, introduced by Dr. Jennifer Mullan in her Decolonizing Therapy Sacred Rage series explains this intergenerational way our epigenetics has "disassociated, restless, and dismissive is an emotional, physical and psychological injury that has been passed down collectively due to genocide, separation, displacement and this has led to sacred grief we have not been safe enough to process". (Sacred Rage webinar).

In her debut book <u>Decolonizing Therapy Oppression, Historical Trauma and Politicizing your Practice</u> Dr Jennifer Mullan writes "There is research tosuggest that dissociation is a spectrum and that many people- particularly for people with colonized histories- detachment from our physical bodies is not only a coping mechanism, but a form of bodily intelligence and safety." Considering the lived historical traumas of oppression and personal attachment wounds like seperation, abandonment, and other sacred losses.

I highly suggest purchasing Dr. Jenn's book and webinars at decolonizingtherapy.com for more.

The Roots of Sacred Rage and Sacred Grief

In keeping with the duality of Marianismo, I want to talk about both the sacred rage and the other part of sacred rage, which could be considered *nice nasty* or straight up direct rage. Now these are often labeled the burdens or the negative traits of Marianismo when they're in the body through the epigenetics, maybe stored from an ancestral place of feeling overlooked, manipulated, taken advantage of. There could be many factors that contribute to sacred rage. Sacred rage looks like "I feel really, really angry. But I know that some of this is mine, but this feels almost like such a big emotion" that you may feel afraid of how you may respond because it feels like it's impacting all the cells in your body and maybe the thing that you feel sacred rage about, yes, it's a big deal, but this right here right now feels like a really big accost, a big front, like something that is threatening your livelihood. So if it doesn't make sense, I invite you to look at the ancestral connection of your sacred rage. Now this could be, you know, somebody limiting your access to resources or opportunities and then you become rageful and you wonder why. But consider that that is an ancestor who has felt that rage and you are now in a better position to discern it, to transmute it, but also to even be aware that you've been carrying this rage for them, deep within you as a reminder of protection of what to notice and how to activate the anger to fight/flight/flee. Maybe whatever has come up to you has unlocked that stored deep abyss of rage. What if you looked

This is where we can get to know our sacred rage, not be afraid of it, I mean, it might feel physically scary, but to really start to ask it questions. Noticing with compassionate curiosity rather than suppression.

One way that I noticed is by saying, well, what's the root feeling? What root feeling am I feeling when I have this rage? When I think about the word sacred, I think it's more than just mine.

And it makes it my feelings sacred. It makes my body a ceremony space to bear witness of this message of activation. It makes it something that deserves to be honored, but also something deeper, which will require much more depth and really bringing it up to surface, right? Pushing the rage down, that hasn't helped. Obviously these ancestors, maybe they did live in rage, but maybe they're reminding you of something in this new issue that has brought up this feeling of rage.
If you think of it like a thread that you found and you just follow the thread, you might find the ball of yarn being, you know, sexual abuse or financial exploitation or somebody who has labored for most of their life and they feel they've been exploited or they never got to rest. And now you're here in this era.

Let's say somebody promised you 20%, or somebody promised you a certain amount from, let's say a collaboration you did. And then at the last minute, they changed their minds and you feel really angry. And rightfully so, right? But this feels like a deep fire that you have felt before.

It might almost feel like an out of body experience, or a fear of maybe I won't be able to control how mad I am. Well, that's where I start to go, wait, what is all this and who else felt this in my life? One example of sacred rage I have felt around exploitation is I remember I was approached by this woman to do an event with my company, Rooted in Reflection.

The Roots of Sacred Rage and Sacred Grief

She was the rep for a local company and said, you know, we'd love to have an event with you and I agreed. It was a great event to be honest. It was beautiful and impactful. I poured my sacred energy into the collaboration and the day of ceremony. I wouldn't change anything from the event. However, once it came to payment, she had changed the script. She had said prior they would only take 20%. And now she was like, you know what, I think I'm going to take 50%. Instantly my rookie mistake was not getting a contract and going off trust in someone that I didn't know to know better than me. The event space that we used was wonderful, but I did most of the work.

I brought in the people, I marketed, I did the day of performance, my husband DJ'ed. I mean, we did the work and to take 50 % after you said 20%, that really got me mad. I will add that the woman is a Caucasian cishet female, & I think that is what made my sacred rage feel guarded. When I tell you, when she suggested that, I felt like somebody had ignited my inner fire and I didn't even know why I felt so angry. It was almost as if I suddenly had a jetpack on, fueled by generations of exploitation and I didn't even know it and the minute she recommended taking 50% my jetpack was lifting me off to lose my mind and I was a little bit aggressive with her which also scared the recovering people pleaser in me. But then I quickly found a middle ground of being a little bit frightening, but very direct. This is a marianismo legacy resource and ancestral takeover from a benevolent baddie. I felt like in that moment, my grandmother spoke for me. She said, Cynthia, calm down, get it together, but be firm. And I was able to calm myself down. I really channeled my ancestors, please help me right now because this is not fair and I don't wanna lose my shit, but I wanna get my money. Because at first when I came at her, I was gonna shake her up. We were on the phone, but I was gonna verbally shake her up a bit because she was messing with my money but they (ancestor) put this stillness and almost like the way that I talked to her was this like calm rational anger that i'd never seen in myself before and it was amazing and I think that was me protecting my sacred rage while also honoring it.

Scarcity Mindset vs Expansive Mindset in Marianismo

Scarcity of love, money and rest has created a sacred rage within. When I acknowledged the root of this feeling of being taken from creatively and energy of spirit and finances, I was able to see my scarcity epigenetics switch on. I have to hold my tummy and bring myself to the space I am in and remind these ancestral cells that the circumstance is not the same and we can advocate for ourselves. On an episode of The First Gen Psychologist with Dr. Lisette Sanchez entitled *Inherited Patterns: Unraveling Marianismo and Scarcity Mindset in Our Epigenetics,* Dr. Lisette and I address how Marinaismo has us in scarcity of our own enoughness. As first gens we often carry this burden of never being good or fast or successful "enough" to make up the pain of sacrifice and suffering our root elders have endured. This impacts our own wellness and lived experiences.

My expansive mindset uses the same abundant creativity and innovation I put into my work and family for my own rest and self care. My expansive mindset reminds me that my ideas are never ending and replenish with my deep dreaming and midday naps. My expansive love brings me into collaborations for the highest good of our art and our legacy. I am enough just being myself and I am abundant in my being. An expansive mindset mothers me to relish in my rest and stretch wide into every inch of my craft as my limitless potential and my sacred time with ancestors.

MARIANISMO PROXIMITY TO SAFETY

This is a visual of the proximity one may feel to be safe enough to show up vulnerable and authentic in the autonomic nervous system

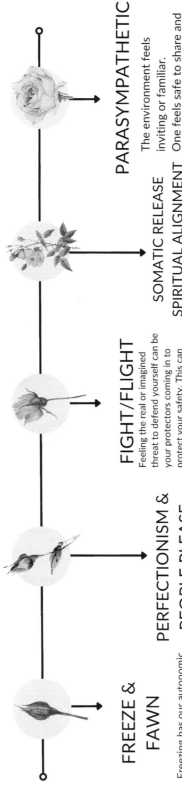

FREEZE & FAWN

Freezing has our autonomic nervous system in dorsal vagal which shuts us down from persistent oppression to be agreeable or frozen

PERFECTIONISM & PEOPLE PLEASE

Feeling the need to get it perfect or be good can be a survival response rooted in lack of safety and fear of scarcity. This can lead to being unsure and disconnected from our autonomy.

FIGHT/FLIGHT

Feeling the real or imagined threat to defend yourself can be your protectors coming in to protect your safety. This can look like criticism, anger, avoidant, and guarded. Your body is feeling ready to escape in the most efficient way

SOMATIC RELEASE
SPIRITUAL ALIGNMENT

A moment feeling into your body and root feelings about the moment. Grounding yourself in your safe breath, movements and aligning your spirit with your most highest good & rituals for self without judgement

PARASYMPATHETIC

The environment feels inviting or familiar.

One feels safe to share and is authentic and in their flow; inviting their creativity and empathy to shine. Adaptable and connected to self, to body and to the present moment.

The wind can be a loving reminder of your innate power and autonomy to move in a safe direction & pivot for your highest good.

Need a reminder of your divine gifts? Spend a moment with the sun on your third eye to show you your ancestral wisdom and body knowledge. You are enough everyday like a sunrise from grandfather sun's safe masculine love. Can the warmth of the sun soften your heart and ignite your fire to stand firm in your Ser?

The land can carry the weight of your grief. Can you allow Mother Earth to hold the impact of your sacred rage on your body with a walk/sit with her under your feet? Can you be with yourself outside and allow your body to feel with the land?

Water is available to hold you, to hear your cries, to pour out of you to release generations of sacred grief. Water can be a loving reminder that you are allowed to feel big like a wave and float until you're ready to swim again.

The moon's love is safety in cycles that allows for all sides of you and loves you every evening until you rise. She meets you at the end of every long day, loving you for past, present, and future you.

copyright rootedinreflection.org

"My mother's heart is in my gut"-- I wrote this in a journal one morning after a vivid dream that felt like an astral projection to my mom's energy.

"Though her soul requires seeing, the culture around her requires sightlessness. Though her soul wishes to speak its truth, she is pressured to be silent."
Clarissa Pinkola Estes
Women Who Run With Wolves

SO NOW WHAT DO I DO WITH THIS ?

If this feels like a whole heck of a lot, you are not alone. This is a lot and that's why our ancestors had protective ways of numbing or disassociation because oppression takes so much of our natural energy that we do what we can. Our ancestral cells and spirit guides are calling upon us now to feel the grief and rage, create safety for it to be witnessed and felt, and then transmute it into a better world for your lineage and the collective.

Our epigentics goes both ways.
Polyvagal toning is basically just saying we tone our autonomic nervous system using somatic tools (aka your body, your senses, the natural elements) to strengthen your nervous system to be in parasympathetic for longer periods of time. This strengthens our nervous system. And guess what?

Your ancestors have BEEN KNOWING THIS! But colonization forced indigenous, Black and Brown peoples to stop displaying their cultural rituals and identities and assimilation was life or death. And yet, our epigenetics proves that while our trauma can be passed on, so can our joy and our connection to nature. Our innate gifts are within us and can also be tones and channeled for our epigenetic flow and our ancestral glow. So do what your ancestors would have done to be in connection with the land, their highest self, their wisest ancestor self. Dance, cook ancestral foods, go outside, cry in safety, swing in the wind, plant a protective garden, build an altar, live like a loving living ancestor. And allow yourself to receive.

Candita
Written By Cynthia Alonzo Perez

I have a little viejita who inhabits space in my spirit
Maybe it's a dwelling in my heart
I started calling her "Candita"
She sits in a small corner of my knowing, in the shadows of scarcity with a small light on at her sewing table
Her coffee has gone cold and her vision blurry from focusing on the thread
Tongue out and foot on the peddle she cracks her knuckles and repositions to produce
Colorful huipiles with birds and flowers created by dawn
Creativity held captive
I see her more clearly now, working for me, for us
Night after night weaving hamacas and marketing them en mis sueños
Never resting herself
It's time to tell Candita to turn the lamp off and head to her own hamaca
And I close my laptop and my eyes and join her

My mother Aurora and her grandmother Aurora "Lola" on her wedding day.

AI generated image of how I imagined my ancestors at the sewing machine.

My Marianismo

Timeless   **POLYVAGAL TONING**   Breaking Cycles

WHAT IS THE TOP DOWN- BOTTOM UP POLYVAGAL TONING APPROACH IN MY MARIANISMO?

"The ability to respond and recover from the challenges of daily living is a marker of well being and depends on the actions of the autonomic nervous system." Porges, S.

Let's look at the three principles of Polyvagal Theory through the lens of Marianismo resourcing and root reactions.

Autonomic Hierarchy-The autonomic nervous system is separated into three tiers of protection that fire off different actions based on the surrounding environment (whether real or perceived). Listed here from top to bottom:

    Dorsal- Freeze mode is the protector that shuts us down, logging off the brain from sending messages or receiving messages from the body. This is a last ditched effort to survive by playing dead, playing nice, shrinking or being perfect as to avoid a terrible fate.

    Sympathetic- This action moves in to fight or flight and move the body into a safer position. Although with past traumas, this automatic reaction may be easily triggered if heightened regularly. The nervous system readies the body for action.

    Parasympathetic/Ventral Vagal- This is our ability for safety and connection through social engagement and co-regulation.

Noticing where you are on this hierarchy most often is an observation at our body-mind connection.

Neuroception- This is our nuanced overachiever informing our autonomic nervous system using information perceived from 1. inside the body, 2. outside environment and 3. person to persons relationships through discernment of these factors. Noticing and being aware of our neuroception is a step in self-compassion and conscious awareness.

Co-Regulation- Our need to feel safe is animalistic for survival, and so is our imperative need for co-regulation. How we have been raised regulated by the adults shapes how we grow to self-regulate. Co-regulation allows our brain the much needed connection to sooth and the sense of a shared, collective safety. Co-regulation is a universal survival need as it mirrors the nervous system state of the environment. When in safe co-regulation, we find ourselves in a flow and able to be reciprocal and empathic.

My Marianismo
POLYVAGAL TONING

"Our nervous system is always trying to figure out a way for us to survive, to be safe."
— Dr. Stephen Porges

WHAT IS THE TOP DOWN- BOTTOM UP POLYVAGAL TONING APPROACH IN MARIANISMO?

Coined by Dr. Stephen Porges, Polyvagal Theory focuses on what is happening in the body and the nervous system, and explains how our sense of safety, danger or life threat can dictate, even activating our behavior. Using methods to source our energy from the top or the bottom of our systems helps our vagas nerve send the systems a message of "todo bien" to self sooth naturally.

Polyvagal Theory gives us a scientific framework that supports the integration of physiological ("bottom-up") therapies with cognitive ("top-down") approaches to help change and improve how we feel, think and connect with others. (Porges, 2009). Self regulating using approaches can be bottom down with your body is on option while regulating your system through top down cognitive support is another. We can incorporate bilateral stimulation and nature for an indigenous ceremony of self.

"It has become increasingly evident that bidirectional interactions between the brain and peripheral tissues, including the cardiovascular and immune systems, contribute to both mental and physical health." Taylor, A., et al C. (2010).

WHAT ARE SOME POLYVAGAL TONING PILLARS IN HEALTHY MARIANISMO?

Top Down

Mediation
Art/Imagination
Glamour Magic
Mantras
Writing
Reading
DJing
Music
Singing
Floating
Showering
Eating
Aromatherapy
Sun/Prana Energy
Humming
Birdwatching
Nursing a baby

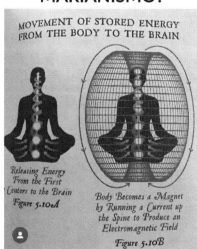

The energy we release top down or bottom up becomes the energy we give to others and representents our internal energetic state.

Bottom Up

Dancing
Stomping
Feet in the water/soil
Grounding
Holding hands
Swaying
Cooking
Walking
Hiking
Gardening
Yoga
Sex
Hammock nap

"With a heart still burdened from a level of loss and grief I'd wish upon no one, Mami mustered the courage, with Eric on her hip, to set out for a foreign land. A nation where she didn't speak the language. A country that provided a haven from the poverty and violence and despair she was desperate to flee. Along the way, she fell down, got up, and then toppled to her knees again. But in the end, she always got up. She crawled back to her feet. She stood. And she deserved not my contempt but my deepest admiration."
― Diane Guerrero, In the Country We Love: My Family Divided

How has marianismo impacted my my relationship with others & myself?

How has my mother's legacy burdens impacted my relationship with myself?
What would the most healed compassionate version of my mother's highest self want for me and my highest good?
What do my most benevolent healed ancestor wish for me?

root legacy letters
Some letter prompts if writing if your process:

a letter to my mother from inside the womb:
a letter to myself from my mother as i am in her womb:
a letter to 1 year old me from my most loving benevolent ancestor:
a letter to baby fetus me from my present self
a letter to my intergenerational highest self from my well and wise ancestor

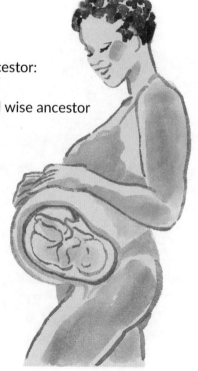

Is Marianismo blocking our chakras? (a question I asked my ancestors)

Marianismo in our chakras

Have you considered yourself enough to consider that Marianismo, your mother's Marianismo at that, is most likely also impacting your auric field by way of blocking your chakras. What could this mean? This could mean we are constantly limiting our own potential because we have a blocked energy field. When we have trauma that has not been cleared out of our cells because they haven't been felt and transmuted or maybe they are unconscious stored trauma in your cells from past generations, regardless, your energy could be blocked preventing your life force energy to be weak or charged with stagnant/negative energy.

What do I mean by this?

I mean, consider your whole being and all that is impacted by not only the 7 generations of trauma you have inherited by your family, but add the daily toxic stress of just paying bills and working daily. Add that stress with the oppression of capitalism and colonialism and your energy is impacted in your physical body, the pace of your thoughts, and the energy fields that are your life for energy or your Prana or Chi energy.
Before doing my own research about chakra energy work or prana energy, I didn't believe in all this stuff and would never have imagined years later I am writing about chakras and the life force energy as an intervention for my healing. And yet, I am so grateful to be on this path for a natural approach to not only self soothing but cellular change for whole body health and it has been a novel and welcomed ritual.

So what am I talking about Marianismo being part of our life force energy?
I am happy to explain but first I will share my personal story with learning about my chakras and balancing my life force energy. My journey started with unblocking my root chakra. I share this story in my next book, *My Marianismo: Energy Healing from Root to Crown*. This is also the name of the 8 week group I host where we have a platica around our marianismo, their marianismo, healed reimagined marianismo and the energy it takes up in our bodies. Each week we honor a certain color, body part and chakra associated with the color. This group came to me in a meditation and showed me the chakras blocked by our marianismo epigenetic trauma. I thanked ancestor and ran inside the house to write up the workbook. I ended the group with a hammock homecoming using the hamacas my aunt gifted me. The same hamacas I had been seeing in my dreams. It was a full circle moment and is still one of my most intimate and sacred offerings. It really is deeply rooted in my lineage to offer my energy in this way.

Back to the roots, for those interested in going deeper, consider energy healing and the energy marianismo takes and adds to your physical and energy body. Pobrecita.

Root chakra carries the trauma of 7 generations before you.
Consider some of the deep lows you may have felt were scarcity in your ancestors times that your present is triggering. How can you separate that energy and clear the home within you at the roots?

The Thorns

The thorns are actually the reasons I wrote this book. Our thorns deserve so much love and space. The thorns are the protectors that never got to be the petals. Obviously they wanted to be soft and bloom, that's why they protect constantly. What can we do for the future generations if we let them explore their sensitive nature without having to fend off or fight?

I was in deep thought about the word *vulnerability* and proximity to safety. One can only be as vulnerable to be authentic determined by the safety they have to disarm. Raising three sons whom are totally different has allowed me to sit in gratitude for the safety to witness a thorn bush blossom into a rose garden. I realize my mom did not have space to be vulnerable because my dad was not understanding of her feelings often or he himself simply did not have the emotional bandwidth to hold it with her. Maybe her emotional crying triggered his own longing for his mother or reminded him of his mother's grief. I hear my grandmother's cried a lot. That is something their children still remember is the sadness and worry the women held. I remember my mom often started an argument at the dinner table. This was most dinners. I actually now see her protectors whereas before I only saw an emotional, irrational woman. She would go to work full time then prepare dinner for all of us and serve my dad live as he sat down. Serving him live meant if he needed another lime for his beer or another napkin to mop up his mustache, he expected my mom to get it and take care of it. This may have triggered my mother's own protectors of resentment for not being able to calmly finish her own meal. Maybe she longed to be sitting with her own parents and she was in another country with no friends and a family that wanted every last piece of her presence. My dad was a loving dad but I believe the two of them together brought out the worst protectors in each other. My dad would often say mean things to my mom about her family. He would remind her how her parents "left her" to go work in the fields and say that's why she acts "como una niña". I remember yelling at my dad when every time he would say those things. My inner protectors have been a first chair defender of my mother and siblings whenever my dad went on his rants about my moms faults. It always felt very sad to feel the emotions they were both throwing each other. She would blame him for being away from her family to live in the states. He would blame her for not being grateful for the children and life they were creating in California, at the dinner table. It is no wonder I remember her often throwing her balled up napkins at the table. I still remember always finding balled up square napkins wherever she sat. She was probably crumbling them up in her pockets as much as she could stand before the outburst overcame her and came over us like high tide.

When I look at my children now I see so many opportunities to support their safe vulnerability. Often times at this age in their childhood protecting their authenticity means being quiet and observing, not chiming in with judgement or comparison. My protectors may want to guard my children from being too chatty or too loud and while those thorns are keeping danger away from the stem, they also transfer a susto of doubt onto my children. When thinking about thorns there is re-claiming to do to soften the thorns. What parts of myself, my mother, my children have had to take center stage and which parts felt pushed into obscurity? Can we be a witness to all the parts of our marianismo and our mother's marianismo with patience? Can we remember the roots as the informant and the thorns as the first line of defense?

My Marianismo Epigenetic impact on the Thorns

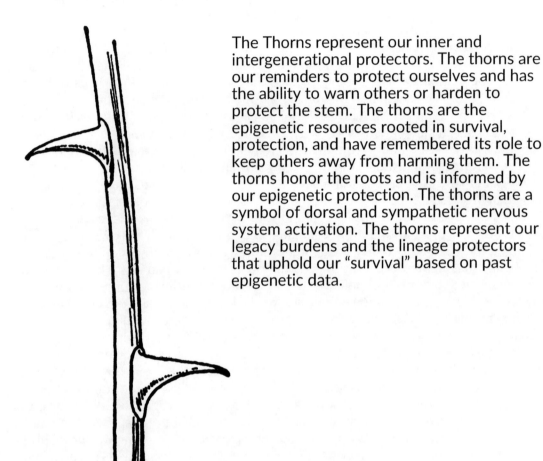

The Thorns represent our inner and intergenerational protectors. The thorns are our reminders to protect ourselves and has the ability to warn others or harden to protect the stem. The thorns are the epigenetic resources rooted in survival, protection, and have remembered its role to keep others away from harming them. The thorns honor the roots and is informed by our epigenetic protection. The thorns are a symbol of dorsal and sympathetic nervous system activation. The thorns represent our legacy burdens and the lineage protectors that uphold our "survival" based on past epigenetic data.

Thorn Protectors can look like
anger, numb, cold, overbearing, skeptical, distrusting, cynicism, resentment, criticism, distant, distracted, busy

Lineage Protectors
The one who overextends, The Scapegoat, The Parentified child, The 'Black Sheep", The Fixer
Historical trauma of immigration can have thorns informed by ancestral attachment trauma, parent/child separation, sacred grief and sacred rage
The thorns impact the heart chakra.

Safety is the root of vulnerability

My Marianismo is seeking safety
My Marianismo can create safety
My Marianismo is my most loving expansive inner mother
My Marianismo is intuituive magic

Have you ever been triggered by something that feels like your reaction is bigger than you? How does your body respond?

How does your body respond when someone offers your help?
How does your body respond when you have to ask other

Stressors in Latinidad

Immigration/Seperation
Money Trauma
Child-Parent loss
mental illness
physical illness
Religion
Adultism
Respecto
Sexism
Shame
Colorism
Violence
Substance Abuse
Education/Language
Seperation/ Abandonment

Autonomic Nervous System Reflexes impacted by Epigenetics

Parasympathetic → Reflect

Flight → Reject

Fight → Protect

Fawn → Perfect

Freeze → Deflect

"The doors to the world of the wild Self are few but precious. If you have a deep scar, that is a door, if you have an old, old story, that is a door. If you love the sky and the water so much you almost cannot bear it, that is a door. If you yearn for a deeper life, a full life, a sane life, that is a door."
— Clarissa Pinkola Estés, <u>Women Who Run With the Wolves</u>

A Conversation with myself

"My Mother Wounds are my Mother's Wounds", this voice said to me as I sat in silence in the rainforest of Puerto Rico. Her past wounds are my present pain. I witnessed in myself a longing for a love I could never get. Picture my home like a toy claw machine, I was always hoping for deep connection, curiousity, time with her, and I always felt like a plushie never picked and her claw was an uninterested weak grab.

How has Machismo and Marianismo played a part in my sacred rage and grief?

Resentment as a protector
Busy as a Protector
Distant as a Protector
Nonchalant as a Protector
Giving, Productive, Overachieving as a protector
Perfectionism and Procrastination as a Protector

Questions I ask myself:

But who are you without the fear of protectors? Who are YOU?? That is what matters.

What wounds are holding you back from your epigenetic freedom to reimagine.

The magic of Marianismo is being in your epigenetic power, a flow, a freedom.

My Marianismo

Timeless   Breaking Cycles

MARIANISMO AS A LEGACY BURDEN

"Your coping behaviors show you what needs witnessing, caring for, and unburdening. If we can just approach them with curiosity and compassion, we might find what is underneath it all."
— Natalie Y. Gutiérrez LMFT, <u>The Pain We Carry: Healing from Complex PTSD for People of Color</u>

WHAT ARE LEGACY BURDENS?

Legacy Burdens
My favorite definition of the term is best explained by my favorite book on complex PTSD in people of color, The Pain We Carry- Healing from Complex PTSD for People of Color, by Natalie Gutierrez, LMFT

"...due to these painful and perhaps prolonged occurrences, you have naturally developed negative beliefs about yourself and the world. These beliefs and the energy accompanying them, are burdens that you internalize and carry within, both consciously and unconsciously, that dictate how connected, protected, and safe you feel-or don't feel."
- The Pain We Carry- Healing from Complex PTSD For People of Color by Natalie Y Gutierrez, LMFT

WHAT ARE SOME LEGACY BURDENS OF MARIANISMO?

Colonized Cultural Expectations of Marianismo

The burden of Marianismo can be so veiled and nuanced because it is a colonized value that moves the womb holder to be the pillar for all before herself and that is her contribution, what she gives and does to help others.

Kind
Nurturing
Sacrifice
Selfless
Virtuous
Maidenly
Supportive
Quiet
Forgiving
Modest
Attractive
Humble
Available for everyone

My Marianismo Legacy Burdens

Rooted in abandonment attachment, wounds due to immigration, vulnerability in relationships is difficult. It feels unsafe to be vulnerable. It might be taken from you. It might be squandered. It might be held against you to be vulnerable. Okay, so those are legacy burdens of marianismo. So I might be cold or not share, I may appear disinterested when maybe I long for connection.

The impulse to shrink.
This one's really big. This impulse to have to be humble, to have to close up, to have to hide and not be seen. Consider that this legacy burden has been passed down to you through your abuelos, abuelas, your mother, your dad, your caregivers, to just disappear, to not be seen. Because think about it, maybe in our parents' generation, maybe it meant they would get in trouble with their parents, they would get beat, they would get punished.

Maybe for their parents, your grandparents or your great grandparents, it literally meant life or death to be seen, to show up, to not be humbled, to be braggadocious. It could have meant death. So we have learned how to disappear, how to be humble, and it is in our DNA. And so think about that now when we're trying to show up as our authentic self and it feels hard and it feels like we're cased in. We have like a casting around our nervous system that's like, "no, no, shrink, staying this small is safest". And it almost like poofs us back. And really just trying to see, my gosh, how has humility kept my people safe in the past? But also how is it keeping me small now? And how do I need to shake it off because it's no longer serving me?

So the impulse to shrink or perform for safety is neuro biological in the energy body, our physical energy body. There is fear of never being enough or never having enough. So this makes us have to perform or chase or do or juggle. And we're always going to be searching for that approval or that celebration from others. Really it's and external validation or superficial co-regulation to let us know that we're connected and we're safe. This is how we stay safe as an animal group but this is also us moving from our reptilian brain.

Perfectionism and over giving as acceptance aka safety.
Competition and Comparison as status aka safety.
Materialism as merit aka safety.
Beauty as assimilation aka safety.

These are burdens because it tends to be taken advantage of. We tend to over-perform or over deliver or be all for our productivity and consider if that is actually doing us harm. Now, if you heard the burdens and you're like, gosh, yes, yes, I know someone that has all of that. Let's look into the legacy resources and re-wire our brains to remember our magic.

Invisible Labor- The Burn Out of Marianismo

In 2017 I found myself restless with what some may diagnose as post partum anxiety but I referred to it as the rebirth of my lineage because wow there was a portal open that was all my ancestral cells forming from me. Living in post partum fog is by far the most surreal lonely soul seeing moment of my life. Sometimes I just picture that new mother I was, laying on the floor crying while my kids stomped on the toy keyboard and clapped along to Mickey. They were safe and happy, but me, mama, was usually not okay. I was coping, white knuckling it, keeping my seam together though I felt myself unraveling. In 2018, My friend Karla and I teamed up to create WellMamaCafe where we held space for topics and togetherness while practicing self compassionate relaxation techniques.

The topic we discussed first was the caregiver burn out as "the invisible load of motherhood". We had 12 women gather as we talked about the mental load mothers carry. As a BIPOC group of mothers we couldn't help but discuss our multi layered intersecting identities and the historical traumas in our own lineages. This topic opened up portals of penance where we conjured up bigger truths.

As womb holders of color, often times we face the invisible labor of motherhood on several fronts. While all mothers carry an important responsibility of mothering the future lineage, they rarely will be acknowledged for all that they juggle in their homes. Add another element in this balancing act like having recently immigrated from a country that speaks another language, add the grief of leaving your own land and family, add the lack of time and space to grieve said losses, add the racism felt through the devaluing of your job and wage, and top it all off with the expectation that this is what you can handle, this is nothing to complain about when your elders "had it worse". So much invisibility in marianismo. Often by society and employers. Likely by educators and policy makers. Sometimes by the medical professional right in front of you who is speaking about you to your English speaking family member instead of calling in a translator to bring you, the expert on your needs, more comfort. Invisibility as comfort for white supremacy. Invisibility as an essential worker upholding capitalism with their skill at withstanding their "unskilled labor". We carry such an invisible labor that is it making us physically sick. It has been coded in our DNA as protection so much that we forget how to take up space. We don't trust our own voice. Far too invisible to even see a way through this grief and discomfort.

When we are invisible to our own family, though, whew, that's a trap. It can feel like no place is safe to bear witness to all your burdens with authentic expression. When we push expectations onto new mothers and judge them instead of offer, we miss an opportunity to support a young ancestor in noticing her own inner magic. When we dismiss or minimize the magic of others we see only value as the laborer they can be. We are so much more than what we do. We are the essence of the home, the pulse and the breath. We are the mirror for how everyone in the home sees themselves. It is because of this that pouring into mothers at all stages of their parenting is vital. Bearing witness to the expansive capacity a woman can grow into with compassionate support is a collective offering.

For all of the wombholders who face multiple intersecting identities that go under the radar, consider that your intergenerational work is simply taking up space, bearing witness to the magic you possess and living a life that is authentic and connected to nature. When you notice yourself, it makes it harder for others to ignore you for your light is too bright.

Guilt and Shame as a Legacy Burden of Marianismo

The whole GUILT THING can feel like physical pain as Marianismo is rooted in feeling guilty for pleasure and sin. I find myself having to pull myself out of this cycle of Marianismo guilt that my epigenetics likes to go on. It likes to go, my gosh, you need to over apologize, over deliver, over sacrifice now because you had an emotion.
What if I can ground myself, come back to myself as human as someone who also might have many needs.

Have I eaten? Did I drink water? Did I explain myself? Did I move my body? What do I need? How can I come back with my resourcefulness and my traditions of showing love?
I can prepare a beautiful meal. I can sit with them and say, hey, I don't like the way this energy was in my body. It didn't feel good to say that to you. And I'm still feeling it. So I can imagine you are too. And I'm really sorry. That's not my intention. And can you forgive me?

I'm able to shift my traditions, whether I receive that or not, I'm able to go, this is the tradition, because I am the mother and I am really standing in this.

And if you're reading this and you're not a mother, this is for you too, because you've had a mother or you have had some kind of lack of need from your mother, if you knew them or if you didn't. We all have a lack of something, some deeper than others. And some, we talk about it all the time. Yeah, I'm mad at my mom for this and I'm mad at my mom for that. And some of us never get to express that anger in their mother, because they feel that they have to be beholden to them or forgiving of them.

This is also something we can go, okay, I'm not a mother, but I feel these things.
Yes, this is for you.

And how about the children of marianistas?

So if you are a male or you self identify as a male, this is for you.

To see yourself as wow, it's not that anything is wrong with me or that I need to stop crying or that it's feminine.

It's that my mom was pushing an agenda out of protection onto me. And that's actually, that's not who I need to be. I need to love myself.

If you identify as someone in the queer community, LGBTQ, and you've felt the real physical pain and a deep lack of authentic safety, being unsafe around your own mother.
I'm so sorry cariño, nobody should have to experience that. And yet I also think about the grief for the mother of like, wow, this is a divine child and mothers are really limiting their majestic flow as a mother by not loving all the essence of their child by trying to change them into something that they're not born to be. What a loss of opportunity for mothers that they choose social conditioning over connection. Of course we can have some empathy but first and foremost comes your safety and freedom to frolic in your truest life.
You're supposed to be in your divine queer magical essence. I feel so bad for that parent that their legacy is small and really living in the burden of marianismo. And they are missing a connection to part of themselves, which is their child. And if you are that child, I just wanna say I'm so sorry. And also, I really do hope in learning about marianismo, you can really work through your own marianismo wounds, these mother wounds projected onto you that are now like your susto responses.

It also helped me see the burden that I cause when I am in my low vibrational marianismo. When I am in bad energy and I snap at my kids without just going away to check myself , to take a nap, now I'm also projecting that powerful energy onto them. And if it's bad energy, that's still that's sticking with them. That's like putting my susto onto them. That is how powerful my energy is. So I want to be really, really intentional about my energy. I think about when someone at work is upset with me how I think of it all night. When I am upset over something my children did whether on purpose or not, the energy in which I communicate my love or disapointment stays with them until I repair it or discuss our narratives and feelings. They are hoping for my loving co-regulation, after all, I am like Mary in their eyes and how I treat them is a reflection of how safe they are to be vulnerable with me.

That is my marianismo legacy to cultivate. What a gift to both my inner child and the women before me who I know long for that because I feel it in me.
When I resource my creative energy, I want to make sure that it's in goodness I want to whip it up como si nada but in a beautiful flow Grassroots energy and collective protectiveness by looking out for others and passing on vital information now. We're really good at Keeping the tea hot but like this is not for me to share. We're good at keeping space, holding space for our comadres, our community, being a safe place for people to go. And we're also good at sharing what needs to be shared with discernment, right? When we're in our highest self with discernment to protect people. Thinking about in our lineage, who were those people that said, no, I don't care if I'm the black sheep. Who was the wild bird who flew away to pursue more out of their living legacy?

My cousin Ileana's daughter Alyssa was the first baby in the family for us to become "tias" in 2002. When she was born her mother was 21 years old and did a wonderful job of raising her and let us all participate in her childhood. Now Alyssa is 21 herself, is talented in many things and a light for everyone around her. This year she applied to go to college in Madrid, Spain and was accepted. She figured everything out herself from how she will pay the tuition to where she will live. Within months of being accepted she was ready to move to Spain. At her going away party at her mom's house we saw so many people whom have been a part of her childhood because her mom always invited us to be, she gave her daughter the gift of collective love. In that moment I healed this guilt part in myself because of the authentic pure pride and excitement I felt for Alyass's upcoming journey. I told Alyssa I now know without a shadow of a doubt that our well and wise ancestors want us to live a joyful, restorative, flavorful life without guilt. They want big things for us for that is what they have always wanted for their lineage. I knew that because of the immense swelling of pride I was feeling for Alyssa for her bravery and resourcefulness. I was in awe of her pivot and professionalism. I knew I would miss her thoughtfulness but knew it was time for her to think only of herself. I learned in that moment that we truly are being rooted for by ancestors as I root for Alyssa and all the dreams she follows in real time and in the future. No guilt, hija, disfruta!

Colonial Marianismo minimizes or allows abuse

This is an area of marianismo that must be dismantled. The survival need to dismiss, avoid, or ignore is the exact pain point to confront. When we ask *who does keeping this family secret serve?* The answer should be one that honors the most vulnerable person in the situation. Marianismo was created as a story sold to us about gender roles shaped like a mythicsm of heroic femininity. Marianismo was created as a role to uphold patriarchy and colonialism, which by its own need to control creates an unfair power dynamic ripe for abuse and oppression.

Throughout my 20 years in education and social work, one big legacy burden to children is the access to abuse that mothers have allowed by avoiding, dismissing, allowing, transferring, enabling and enacting. While I understand that the way we protect sexual predators is rooted in our own trauma responses, it is also rooted in our cultural norms and hierarchal values. We have been taught not to question adults, that children exaggerate or are too needy. As a therapist I have heard countless stories of mothers with their own inner child trauma and colonial marianismo who do not believe their children's stories of sexual abuse and turn their children into the identified family home wrecker. When mother's abuse their children, it creates a soul loss in the child with confusion around their body and soul safety. The shame inherited in the epigenetics may create a dorsal vagal activation of numbness, disassociation and freeze response to our child's crisis. It may be a pattern we are repeating by the way our beliefs have shaped our autonomic nervous system.

The manifestation of sacred rage may allow for physical abuse from others or from the mother herself. I have heard stories of mothers choosing the step dad's comfort over the safety of the children. When I hear the mother allowing men to hit or humiliate their own child I see the mother's own inner child feeling shame that their own children represent a broken part of them and therefore need this punishment in some way to keep themselves deserving of this man in their life. It is a projection of their own inner child's longing for a paternal figure and if their paternal figure was volatile and abusive, well that is likely who their inner child has picked for their children's parent. Intersecting childhood abuse with the crossroads of immigration and financial survival, this dynamic sets a mother up for familiar epigenetic patterns of fawning and people pleasing within Marianismo. Until someone stops it and says, "Ya basta! Not my children. No more! I can do this without you and I will".

I

I have heard many many many stories of women leaving abusive situations and protecting their children. I have heard it from the perspective of the present child, the adult child, the young mother and the older mother, and all of these stories fill my heart with awe and hope for us. We have endured so much just in our epigenetic DNA and our body holds all the pathways of our survival and our craft.

Many mothers have re-mothered themselves with ancestral love for connection to food, artistry, community, volunteering, and re-connecting with the soft part of themselves that used to be hidden by design. There are generations of cycle breakers before us that although their one switch in direction may seem small like choosing to be a single parent or choosing not to be a parent and be a loving guardian tia, these cycle breakers carry within them a fire that burns down the path to abuse and keeps their warmth for connection to children and animals of the land. That is a marianismo legacy to uphold. The paradigm shift is bringing abuse out of the shadows and clearing the names of the ancestors before us who were put in inconceivable positions of self-betrayal or enabled harm to children. When we stand in our power to say, "no, I wont hide this abuse for you", we give a sacred limpia to our lineage 7 generations past and 7 generations forward.

Marianismo as FOMO and sacrifice, resentment and rage.

FOMO or "The Fear of missing Out" as a Marianismo symptom rooted in ancestral attachment connection and abandonment.

It was in moving past being annoyed of my mother's constant FOMO and difficulty making a decision on where she wants to go and never truly being satisfied that I realized FOMO is rooted in colonization and the trauma of the immigrant abandonment wound. The fear of missing out could have very well have been missing out on food, resources, or safety in our ancestor's life.

On the flip side, it may be difficult to move out of a sympathetic response of constantly sacrificing and staying under the radar, that missing out has become the epigenic flow and taking up space is the challenge.

The root feelings of longing and disenfranchised grief in humbly missing out can create resentment that festers from lineage to lineage with sacred rage spilling out in moments of transformation, intuition, or protection. These are feelings that needed to be uprooted, felt, mourned, yelled, exhalted and within your own process, transmuted into craft, compassion, rest, intuition or whatever else you step into when you shed the sacred rage of 7 generations back.

When I think of compassion for my mother, I think of her FOMO and how that is one of the most difficult things to be patient with her about. She always wants to be everywhere, with everywhere, all the time. I kid with her and call her the name of the amazing movie "Everything Everywhere All at Once", not only is it a spot on title for the Marianismo energy body, but it is a fantastic movie that is worth watching a few times. My mom longed to be here, there and nowhere all at once. She longed to be wherever her children invited her or she would straight up invite herself. Yeah sometimes it was cute but many times it was evasive, controlling and down right inconsiderate of my boundaries. She wanted to be "there" in a sense that when she was with us, "where she wanted to be", even then she was restless, absent in prescence, preoccupied with what others were doing back home, and longing to be invited "there" by "them" whomever "them" was in any space where she felt like she didn't belong or was not invited. I say she wanted to be "nowhere" because even though we did take her, she wanted to be nowhere but home with her mother in Merida, Yucatan. As a child nothing I did was ever cute enough, perfect enough, funny enough to keep her attention on me. She wanted to be nowhere but with her own mother and I was there feeling like nowhere was the only place I could be near my mother.

I know my inner child feels sadness for the intimacy and vulnerability they didn't get in childhood because my mother had difficulty truly seeing me beyond her own sacred grief. Now as a mother myself, I feel sadness for my mother for missing out on moments to truly know me and what fascinates me. I transmute this FOMO into being mindfully present and loving to my children in the moments they or I long to share in vulnerability with them. I don't want to fear missing out anymore, I want to be present and witness the moment.

The Parentification of Marianismo

The parentification of colonized ancestors of the post Hispanic colonial diasporas has not been cared about enough to call it *parentifcation* but rather, "obedience and responsibility". A noble sacrifice that has become a twisted rite of passage. While white American children got terms like parentification, we got punished if our younger siblings got hurt or went without as if it was our responsibility as a child only a few years older than them. This is a lack of accountability by emotionally immature and historically traumatized adults who happen to become parents.
I started realizing how I myself as a first gen therapist didn't even realize I too was parentified until 10 years as a therapist. I didn't give myself the title because that was just a part of our culture to sacrifice something of ourselves everyday and give gratitude for those who sacrificed before us. It's a very Catholic state of self punishment under the guise of a spiritual walk.

I noticed because I was a fat teenager I wasn't treated like a young lady or a growing girl deserving of softness and protection. I was blamed for my weight and disorganized routine and expected to just know how to do things without being parented on the how. I started to notice my parents were like magnets for each other's worst traits. They argued daily and often my mom focused more on her compulsion for activating my dad through arguments and reckless spending, rather than her focusing on mothering us. Being seven years older than my younger brother Marcel, I started caring for him, for us, around age 10. I would take him into my room when they argued. I would make us meals. I would scold him for being sloppy or dirty and give him big sister lectures on social norms around hygiene and manners. I felt sacred anger at my parents for not teaching my brother these important values and lessons. Whenever my dad tried to be stern with my brother my mother would be defensive, this was my mom's trauma response. This usually caused them to argue. I felt grief for us. I also just naturally stepped into a caregiver role when I was around him.

It was just this year in my mother's old age I felt the resurfacing of sacred rage and sacred grief around this parentification wound. Not only did I feel over-parented by my dad, I also felt under-parented by my mom. I felt betrayed by my own mother when she often chose her siblings over us, her children and her husband. This happened often with my dad and her which was a cause for many of their arguments. My mother felt she had to always defend, protected and provide for her 6 siblings. I received the impact of this throughout my life with nuanced displays of being forgetable, dismissed, and unimportant once her family was involved.
This year as she turned 72 I realized she has trauma bonds with her siblings rooted in attachment trauma of immigration and parental abandonment. I do not blame my grandparents for what we may call abandonment. In the 50's my grandfather would leave his wife to go pick fruits in Oxnard, CA as he learned through his own immigration to California as a teenager. Once he was a parent of two babies, my tio Juan and my mom Aurora, he made it a career of being a seasonal farmworker or campesino. He was often gone half the year and would come back and my grandmother would get pregnant and he would leave again.

IMy mom says she believes her dad got her mom pregnant to keep other men from flirting with her while he was away. My mom held some sacred rage towards her father for how her mother struggled to care for seven children under the rule of his controlling and possessive machismo. Once my grandmother was then part of the family work in Oxnard and had to leave her children in Merida with their grandmother and aunts, the siblings became brother dads and sister moms.

This trauma bond within the inner child has left them with loyalties to their siblings are parents and also intimate witnesses of the sacrifice of children of immigrants. The loss of their parents warmth and the burden of parentification through survival and protection of themselves above all. I get it now but it still impacts my intimacy with my mom as mother-mentor.

The sibling burden of Marianismo

Whether trained to be la hija buena or shamed as the hija mala, the way marianismo impacts siblings relationships is equally as important as acknowledging how it impacts our intimate relationships.

I have heard so many stories of the overbearing oldest daughter that carries the weight of the mother and is often second in command for her younger siblings. Often never given time or space to fall apart herself, the oldest feels the marianismo burden of having to keep it together for everyone.

The middle daughter is often the peacekeeper and their essence is considered "soft skills" yet their compassion is the glue of the family. The mother may project her own insecurities onto the sensitive middle child by minimizing their talents and sparkle. The middle daughter may turn against their own intuition to be less themselves and more of what their family needs, someone to keep hustling.

The youngest daughter may be the holder of generations of deep guilt and the burden of the responsibility to "stay home for the family". Whether for economic reasons or emotional manipulation, often the youngest daughter is molded to be catered to, even to their own detriment, They have witnessed the shame and scapegoating their older sisters went through and their own way of coping may be to become less standoutish. To be mediocre and fall under the radar as to not activate the parental protectors of anger and rage the other siblings have received. A victim of vicarious trauma and helplessness, the youngest daughter may feel this big burden of not getting a choice in their life with the legacy burden of having to take care of mom or dad because everyone else is gone.

Add in sons to this sibling mix and the dynamic changes the homeostasis. Sons of marianistas have stated they are treated differently by their moms with a learned helplessness of being told that a woman should do things for them rather than they learn it for themselves, they should be tough while the woman is the only one allowed to be emotional, and they inherit the legacy burden of feeling responsible for the safety and protection of all in their home. This can create a hierarchy and competitive spirit in the home that is not expansive and rooted in machismo. A mother may teach her sons to marry overbearing women then get mad when they do and are loyal to them as the center of the home.

The sibling burden of Marianismo

Queer children also face the burden of toxic marianismo by simply being their authentic selves.

Queer children are a gift to the family lineage as an intergenerational changemaker that confronts our paradigms and encourages us to shift them through love and authenticity. As mothers we are the creators of life and to treat our children as if something is wrong with them is to dismiss our own magic as a creator. Breaking gender norms by choosing authenticity is the gift they invite us to share. Our queer children are a beacon towards our own consciousnesses and offers us a chance to raise our vibration to witness that they are exactly who they are meant to be. That challenges all our beliefs on how we were conditioned to believe what Spirit loves like. Love is actually not tough, love is not shameful, love is expansive and remembers the vastness of nature's love. We do not have the right to get in the way of their divine timing and purpose. Our role is to protect their inner light and learn from them.

If you have a sibling in which you feel resentment towards for advantages or privileges they received above you, there may be another perspective you can look for to understand their own role and burden in the family.

The Nice Nasty of Marianismo

Rooted in resentment which is rooted in Sacred Grief or Sacred Rage of who they have had to be and/or who they never got to discover themselves becoming, there is this double edged sword of marianismo wounds. The perfectionist protector may harbor resentment at having to always be accomodating, graceful, put together and exceptional while others parade around rebellious, haphazardly, authentic.

I couldn't always put my finger on this way marianismo shows up until my friend Raenisha named it one day. "Oh Black people call that NiceNasty, like the church elder who is saying mean things in a nice way, they are acting nasty but play it off with grace so they don't appear mean". This was in response to me sharing my story of this confrontation at the park. One day I went to a playground we frequent because my kids love the zipline at this park. We got to the park and I remember being mindful of spending time being present with them because I had been working so much. I pushed my kids on the tire swing and they were in a happy playful mood. After about 10 minutes I went to the grass to be on our blanket when my mother's doctors office called me so I took the call. While I am listening to the MD I see my kids run to the zipline to "zip". Miles age 7 went first and zipped across. As he went back to the base to hand the zipline to his brother Malcolm whom was next in line, I see this woman walk up to Miles and snatch the zipline from my son and sit her daughter on the zipline and send her off. I am in a moment of disbelief and thought to myself, you didn't just see that, let's wait and maybe the woman didn't see your kids waiting. I watch and she ignores my kids again and zips her child across a second time. By this time my nervous system is in sympathetic mode because since healing my dorsal inner child, my inner mother be protective af. I walked down to the zipline and started telling the woman, "excuse me, excuse me, my kids were on the zipline and you ignored them, excuse me". I was a foot away from this mother and she acted like I was invisible. I said "please tell your daughter to give the zipline to my kids now, hello? do you hear me?" The woman had positioned her body to ignore me and when I felt I couldn't get a response I said, "tell your daughter or I will" and I start to walk over to the girl. The mom finally says, "I am not going to talk to you when you are acting angry like that". My head could have exploded. I was now being shamed by this mom for showing emotion while she ignored me and was ignoring my children and teaching her child this sneaky way of acting on the playground.

The Nice Nasty of Marianismo

The Nice Nasty of this mom was her entitlement, her tone policing of all of us, and her resentful inner child casting spells on all of us. "Your kids were mean to my daughter on the tire swing", she says. My body instantly calmed down because I didn't believe her.

The thing is, I know my kids, I homeschool them, we were raised in a pandemic and are with each other 24 hours a day. "How were they mean to your daughter?" "She asked them if they speak Spanish and they said a little bit. She asked if she can play with them on the tire swing and they said 'not right now, we are playing something together'. My daughter came back crying." I looked at my kids faces, afraid I was going to scold or punish them. She was saying this "calm" as if it was holier than my justified anger.

 I saw her clearly in that moment, her inner child demanding all the children play with her because maybe she had to. I heard myself firmly say, "i know my children werne't mean to your daughter. They are shy kids because we homeschool and they are shy about their Spanish. They also don't have to play with everyone if they choose not to. They are playing Mario & Luigi together and they don't have to stop what they're doing to play and them be made bullies for having autonomy. You on the other hand stepped into children's business and physically snatched and prevented my kids from playing on the zipline. You are acting like a big bully." She started to laugh and say the way my emotions were was angry and all I saw was how she truly believed that though she employed other protectors like dismissive, avoidant, manipulation and vengeful with a docile demeanor, she thought she was right. She was nicenasty and was the playground tone police of Marianismo. My kids still tell the story of how that woman's energy made them, "feel frozen, confused and invisible".

Healing My Marianismo is Shadow work

We are one year into this ongoing active genocide in Gaza by Israel which is modern day colonization our ancestors know. We are witnessing epigenetic trauma in real time. That is why Palestine is freeing us in our colonial minds by pulling the veil down to see what the roots. When I start to feel this big fear, you know, as we're in this economic upheaval, when it feels very scary with upcoming elections and as an American feeling disgust for our country, of our economic status, I take a big deep breath and hold my tummy and my heart with my eyes closed listening for the answer in the moment.
"Ancestors, this is really rocking the way that that we have been told to succeed or to show up." I get this inner knowing & the duality of that inner knowing is my ancestral wisdom, **do you know where your people are from? You can survive and you can create with few resources**. And in fact, Cynthia, when you find your resources, you make abundant resources. **That's who your people are.** And I was like, word? **Yes, that's who we are.** As I allowed that awareness to unravel, I realized, yes, It has found me and I am claiming it.

My marianismo shadow work brings to light the surpressed grief of scared loss of children as babies, as fetuses and as dreams never realized for myself and many parents in my lineage. I can feel their fear over losing another person they love and that ,makes us frozen. I think of my Tia Candita whom who could not conceive children so her husband left her and had children with another woman. She was then the aunt whom was to the go to for babysitting and child rearing whether she was in sacred grief or not, Her sorrow, I carry it with me and when I had my 3 miscarriages, I felt her despair. I had learned through genetic testing that I carry double strands of the MTHFR genetic mutation which is a blood clotting mutation that creates miscarriages by cutting off oxygen to the placenta through clotting. Could my body be an epigenetic protector from my ancestral timelines? Could my body be in sacred grief and my womb clotted before I leaned into indigenous healing like sobadas, accupuntures and limpias? Maybe it was there for me to find it and heal it with my mothering of the 3 sons I have?
My marianismo is not just the negative and I'm so sorry. I'm so sorry if I have been in my anger pocket to think that it's only the bad. In being marianistas of our legacies, we have also created the good, the ability for us to navigate our resources, to change the energy of our environment. It has become a craft. It has become the epigenetic flow of marianismo that I want to be more in.
Because while it has been my survival, my marianismo, I don't need to get rid of all of it. It kept me aware. It kept me ready. I also have these soft Marianismo parts of me that maybe haven't been used so much. The epigenetic switches that are like, hey, I know it's been unsafe for you to be soft and tender and just observant of love & that has caused you to not be able to receive all the love from the people you've helped. But you have this duality in you and it's capable and it's enough to remind you of the love that you carry. I hope that in knowing all of your gifts and your inherited genetic intuitive knowings, you also start to see like, wow, this is me and me is powerful as fuck.
Acknowledging and welcoming all the parts of your marianismo, simply just observing it for now and really just saying, okay, this is what I carry. And also do I want to carry it or am I willing to let it go now?

Post Partum Depression and Anxiety — Epigenetics as a protector

When I say this legacy work of diving into Marianismo in our Epigenetics found me, I am not kidding. I have been living alongside my own lived and embodied research on this topic.

I did not understand epigenetics until I was on the other side of my post partum depression. I wrote this book because I wish I had known these words and the history to see myself on the pages because my children did not deserve the low vibrational energy I carried for the first 4 years of their life.

When I read about epigenetics, I saw myself, I saw my mother, I saw several grandmothers and I felt their sacred grief as a portal with answers. I talk about this in more detail on my podcast Confetti All Around, specifically Season 3 Episode 4 "La LLorona: Not Dead But Not Alive Either" where I discuss the stories we know of La Llorona & Sacred grief & longing.

It was one day when I felt like this post partum fog had lifted I was able to feel clearly; deeply. I thought about African women brought to the America's against their will, separated from their lands and families and violently sold into the oppressive system of white supremacy and enslavement. I had a meditation where I could hear and feel the pain of a Black mother in a crowded, sweaty, labor auction where people were being sold as property for labor. This meditation was intense. And I felt the sacred rage of a Black mother whose child was being "sold" and separated from her. This feeling shifted as my body received this information. As I allowed my third eye to show me more, I felt the deep drowning feeling of grief that rolled in like the fog I had only recently noticed in my new maternal energy body. And lastly, the most daunting and noticeable feeling I witnessed was the numbness. Some may call this feeling "The Knowing Field" and I realize I was a witness to a historical trauma of many wombholders and the feelings passed down and transforms due to its environment.

The disassociation I felt witnessing this tragic man-made trauma of separation, dehumanization, and root pain. I came out of that meditation crying and understood, with deep compassion and tribute, to Black, Indigenous, colonized women who have been taken or forced off their own lands or stripped from their children as if propagating a plant. I saw why post partum can serve as a protector in our ancestral code.

Post Partum rage, post partum numbness, postpartum anxiety, postpartum psychosis. I get it. I am so sorry to past me who didn't understand and to the ancestors within me who were giving me protection that may have helped them in THEIR time, in their situation. I gave it back and worked on what WAS MINE, AND I liberated US.

When having a baby, a portal is opened. This is not only a rite of passage into your divine self but this is an opening to your ancestral traumas and wisdom. I am sorry if we have had our stories severed or lost in colonization. And yet the nervous systems remembers.

Happy ending: This week I went to a store I frequent. The cashier was s a Black elder and when she asked me if I would have another baby I shuddered and said, "I feel too guilty about how out of it I was when my babies were babies. I even apologize to them now for not feeling well then. They tell me I don't need to apologize to them anymore but I just feel so much guilt". She said to me in such a healing protective way, "Guilt has not space in motherhood. There is no time for guilt as a mother. Just show up better everyday with love for them. Stop apologizing and BE present. Who you should apologize to is HER. Apologize to yourself. She deserves it." I have chills just finishing this sentence. We shared loving eye contact and I thanked her with my hand over her hand. She mothered me up that evening. That's community care for mothers.

What are some inner protectors of marianismo?

To be clear, Marianismo, historically, has been imposed on wombholders and self identifying women. Whether we are taught it through discipline, ridicule or rejection, we know the ways to move in our cultura to keep us "surface level safe". This is a loving and honest invitation to go deeper than the surface and into what protector energy shows up to keep our space safe and our eco-systems in homeostasis.

What are the "symptoms" of having to live in the susto response of Marianismo?
Some of us may have difficulty asking for help, asking for more, advocating for self because we have been told we are a burden, we expect too much, we should just be grateful. So our well meaning protectors and our fear sniffing autonomic nervous system want to ensure we never feel that discomfort again so they remind us to play small and quietly in the corner as a sure safe bet.

I encourage you to write down a list of all your protectors that work for you to uphold these Machista and Marianista paradigms. I ask you, what do they take away from you and how do they misrepresent what you truly long for? Sit with this page as long as you need. What do you give up in yourself to uphold these protective roles? What would they need to believe from you to know they can disarm from protecting?

Scarcity as a protector- Our mothers and grandmothers may have had to work really hard to literally have "enough" to eat, "enough" to pay, "enough" labor to work harder, "enough" rest to get back to productivity. While the last 3 generations of mothers in our lineage may have a scarcity around not having enough (material things, family status, finances, etc), our generation often suffers from scarcity as a protector, as a belief of not BEING enough. Scarcity in our worth dictates so much of what we feel deserving of and how much we have worked for something rather than remembering we are worthy just for being, we are exceptional as who we are. It is captialism and white supremacy that has turned our hard labor into a scarcity of our worth. The invitation to this protector in our root and sacral chakras is to move away from being more and sit with the discomfort of already being enough. Being born enough. Imagine that. Imagine them within you feeling born "enough". Can this protector move away from scarcity and into creativity? Think orange, think your inner child. Now, can your creative inner child help scarcity detach and soar into your expansive self? What would that look like?

Humility/Invisibility as a Protector- Humility is well intentioned and noble, sure, but at the cost of whom? When we shrink ourselves so often we become invisible to our selves, that is now our body and spirit performing out of a susto response from past trauma to remain docile, agreeable and calladita to be safe. Can you sit with the discomfort of showing up for yourself authentically- whatever feelings you wake up, making time, clearing the table and all your plans to really be an audience to your humility and ask them what their humble protector is protecting us from? Who would you be in your rawest lows and how would you like to be celebrated in your proudest moments? Can you be your own audience at first? Unblocking your throat chakra often enough to advocate for yourself in big and nuanced way is the "doing".

How could this invisible protection begin to be seen? What parameters could this protector ask for to reveal parts of themselves they haven't witnessed or allowed others to witness? Is there a safe person that is a witness of your parts with out expectation?

What are some inner protectors of marianismo?

Jealousy as a protector- Jealousy is a common feeling when we are not living in our Ser. When we see others creating, dreaming, advocating for their authentic self, it can feel like an offense, their joy can feel like a threat to our protectors. Jealousy feels draining because it is performing from a blocked solar plexus that spreads to the heart and throat to protect our own spot. Jealousy is actually a root feeling of longing, what is this behavior longing for? Can you give it space to express? Can you create the eco-system you need that nurtures your personal sacred blossom? Can you meander in your own garden and tend to the parts of you that long to be seen by you? When jealousy feels tended to, witnessed without criticism, does "jealous" move from protector to a memory of another part of yourself? Can we be a witness and warmth to jealousy so gently that it forgets of others and sees its own beauty?

Busy as a protector- Okay queen, booked and busy and making moves. We see you! When the protectors stay busy, what else do they keep us too busy to tend to? How is our ability to work hard and stay "busy" a distraction from feeling our emotions? How has busy beliefs kept us from rest? Whom or what would you have to finally address with out the protector of "staying busy"?

Disassociation as a protector- Disassociation is a powerful survival tool to protect us from the emotional harm on a neurological cellular and somatic level. While this protector has gotten our ancestors and us through unimaginable harm, it is also keeping us from living the life we have worked so hard to create. When we disassociate from the mundane rituals, we may miss opportunities to notice how plants and animals co-live with us. We may miss the way the wind kissed the top of our head when we cried that we are lonely. We may be wasting our time in relationships that cause us to stay small because our protectors swoop in for the classic disassociation response. Can you create a new protector from this ancestor protector? What is this protector which helps you stand up from yourself to "dis-associate" yourself from those whom you have outgrown? Can you shape shift your protector as the one who helps you detach from others and attach to your present self? What age does this protector feel?

Resentment as a protector- I didn't understand my anger until I spent time listening to my resentment as a protector. Resentment on the surface is anger at others while resentment under the surface is resentment at self for not protecting our own energy, our own peace of body and mind (obviously being forced into unsafe abusive or oppressive situations is the resentment at abusers and is not to be minimized or self- blamed). Energetic resentment protectors are there because they are signaling to our bodies when we are over-extending, over-promising, rapidly shrinking to put the needs of others first. Resentment longs not to be a protector, resentment longs to soften and rest in healthy discernment and realistic boundaries. Can you ask your resentment what body part in lives in and what messages it has for you? Can you ask your benevolent ancestor for energetic and spiritual protection rituals?

Perpetuating Marianismo Thorns

I didn't understand it until my late 30's but also as Dr. Lydiana Garcia has told me, just because we can understand why doesn't excuse it. Marianismo thorns have served in colonialism as a way of peer socialization into obedience of social norms. We may have been raised in a cis-het home where machismo was the first and final word and our body remembers. Raised by a single mother or single father may have developed different thorns for protection. These are personal to our childhood experiences which have had notable consideration on the influence our other environments have on us.

From our cousins, tios, friends, classmates, teachers and eventually, coworkers, we may have received mixed messages about what it means to be a "good girl" or a "strong woman". When considering our thorns, it is a moment to practice reason and re-pair with the parts of us we have had to hide, scold, or abandon to fit these unrealistic gender constraints calmly called "norms". Normal for whom?! When we give rules on ways to show up as a "woman" we limit our full expansiveness.

When we have fellow wombholders telling us how to date, how to dress so we DO get attention then shaming us for how we dress when we do get attention, it may feel like the vibes are off because they are! The thorns of Marianismo serve to protect the immediate eco-system. That can look like good friends suggesting you go on a date with someone whom your gut is screaming at you to stay away from. It can look like friends teaching you to "pre-game" by drinking as social lubrication as a "norm". Maybe it is your co-worker shaming you for wearing your outfit a little too cute and her hater aura is a bit jealous of your grand audacity so to bring you back into the gender dungeon they drag you by your marianismo roots of guilt and shame.

Competition and comparison

These two values have been modeled to us by tias who compare us to our other cousins or by our mothers who are in competition of whom is the best matriarch by the "success" of their children despite the cost of their authentic relationship with them. When we are operating from a place of competition and comparison, we are moving from the ego and ingrained colonialism. When we do this we activate our autonomic nervous system into a sympathetic state for the perceived survival of the current social situation. Social capital has been the root for survival and advancement.

But what about when we move from a place of **Compassion and Connection?** Imagine your heart with a warm green light circling around you and opening you up to your own energy source that is unmoved by the social contracts of others and seeks connection through authentic and vulnerable relationships. Imagine the eco-system you can cultivate when you allow yourself to be of your own heart and show others by standing in your deeply rooted SER.

Production and perfectionism

Did you know the Spanish Viceroy made indigenous people perform religious dances in front of the church to show worthiness? They were to be entertainment and obedience for the Spanish living in the lands they colonized. This need to entertain or be a perfect worker or host, it has seeped into our survival genes and confused us on our genuine personality. I know many of us have been praised for our ability to produce swiftly, abundantly and better than most. Most don't ask HOW we do it (or acknowledge the pain or self-rejecting our bodies natural needs to meet this capitalistic quota) but instead ask for MORE and EXPECT IT. What if we imagine us detaching from this inherited burden of earning our worth through our DOING and relished in living in our inherent worth just by BEING. Think about how many days and years we have lost knowing our quirky, silly, spirited, intuitive self because we were chasing the goals of the oppressor. What if we build a relationship with our imperfect parts and let them show us what our craft is when deeply rested, deeply respected, deeply rooted in our own divine timing. Disfruta!!!

My Marianismo vs. Their Marianismo through storytelling and reflection

Sometimes marianismo is nuanced and calculated. While maybe subconscious, our marianismo has been weaponized and also turned into our own sword. We have been historically turned against each other be it to produce more, to work faster than, to attract status. We have been used as competition in a capitalistic economy dictated by white supremacy. We may have grown up hearing contradicting complaints on our appearance like mom constantly reminding us to put some makeup on and brush our hair, maybe add some earrings, or else what will people say? Dad might walk in the room and scold us for wearing too much makeup and looking like a "puta". Depending on his machismo intensity he either shames with name-calling and yelling or maybe he's the silent heavily burdened machista dad and his face of disappointment says it all.
It's a lot to be raised in these double standards that don't benefit men or women.

We have been raised learning how to navigate marianismo and machismo from the adults we studied. We have become cunning at shapeshifting so much it could be considered a craft to fans or manipulation by foes. Regardless, we have had to be quite crafty, cute and creative to survive the harsh world of being expected to act above our pay grade in every room we exist in. So we become slick at betrayal and trust is not always promised as it was not always given to us in the first place. We become the adult children of ancestrally traumatized inner children parading as our adults. We are longing. We may be seeking true connection but also not open to truly receive it. And that longing may turn to jealousy, envy and even straight up misery.

I think about moments when I feel confused about what is coming from a place of intuition or nuanced vibes. What is mine and what is their marianismo? It helps me personally to call it out in my mind. From 2021-2024 I was fortunate to have a contract through the Eva Longoria Foundation grants that hired me to do tele-health therapy for farmworkers in Central CA and their families. This was a full circle moment as my own mom and grandparents were farm workers in Oxnard and in the same fields of Santa Cruz where my clients were calling from. In this life changing role I was able to discuss the impact of Marianismo in their life and what I learned was how common this is. I knew it was in our genes but these stories, they are the proof.

We often talked about what was their own marianismo and what was being projected or socialized onto them. A client had been working through her feelings of guilt at being in a happy relationship with her baby's daddy. He worked hard to pay for everything so she could stay home. This bothered her mother whom was always bothering her to get rid of him and be single. The client felt confused why her mom wouldn't be more supportive and why she would want her daughter to struggle and be lonely. After discussing Marianismo the client shared that her own mother was a single mother and didn't have any men to help her. She realized she was the same age her mother was when she had her baby and her mother was subconciously projecting how her own experience with her motherhood went onto her. I supported this client by witnessing her own understanding that this energy was her mother's longing and regret playing out. The client's own marianismo was the guilt she felt to uphold her mother's feelings above her own and ultimately above her daughter's. She felt this was becoming an intergenerational pattern. When we talked about the epigenetic protectors activating- she was done, she was ready to face her own lineage and do what her intuitive inner mother knew was best.

My Marianismo vs. Their Marianismo through storytelling and reflection

I think in sharing stories it is important to share some of my own marianismo stories. Truth be told I have many stories and hope to share them in a follow up book I am writing on Marianismo and energy healing. Hey, don't be surprised at the other projects, I am the granddaughter of multitaskers and busy bodies.

When thinking about "their marianismo" I think about a story of friendly betrayal. This is my own story. I was friends with sisters, let's call them Blanca and Eve. Blanca and I were the same age and Eve was her older sister. Our mothers were friends and gathered for fiestas and pozole on Sundays when available. I was lucky to grow up in a neighborhood with other immigrant and first gen families that shared their experiences with us. Blanca and I walked to school together from 6th- 7th grade. I noticed one week she was teasing a boy in school. He was shy and kept to himself, he was very smart and yet people treated him like he wasn't; like something was wrong with him for everything about himself. I had been in that position myself and when I saw the boy, Terrance, I was friendly and kind. The next week Blanca hands me a note from a "secret crush" and she said someone gave it to her to give to me. She was giddy and insisted I read it. Blanca knew I never had a boyfriend and while all my friends were already "scamming" behind the gym, I had never even talked a guy more than friends. I was 50 pounds overweight with a curly mop and blackheads on my round nose. The first thing I noticed was this "admirer" had horrible writing, grammar and tact. Seriously, the penmanship was hard to read and the words were so misspelled I couldn't understand the letter clearly. Either way, the note said this secret person liked me and I forget the details but it asked me for a note in return. So Blanca insisted we write a note. I'm not sure if I did or didn't. What I did learn soon after one more letter from my "admirer" was this was not a love note, it was in fact, a prank. I realized Blanca had been the mastermind teenage marianista behind this "love connection". She had been writing letters to Terrence from me and writing me notes from Terrance and laughing at both of us. Funny enough, the horrible writing and grammar gave her away. When I confronted her she laughed it off and acted like it was nothing. This was the last day I ever walked to school with Blanca. There was such a sick feeling in my body in the way she could have me over for sleepovers one day and the next write fake love notes and being a fake person. That's all I saw after that day. That was Blanca's marianismo, what some may call a meddler, drama, two-faced, toxica, fake, jealous, y metiche.

Now I wish it was an easier breakup when I broke up with her older sister, Eve. Eve was the same age as my older sister but they didn't really get along and my marianismo at 18 was that I liked that about her. Heehee. I think my teenage marianista was looking for a fun friend and a big sister to teach me how to be a single young college girl. My sister was always with her boyfriend and his band, Nobody Cares. That was the band's name, Nobody Cares from Long Beach and throughout high school we went to many of their shows because my sister was with Brian the trumpet player. I swear every friend I brought around the band hooked up in some capacity with someone. There have been babies and marriages and divorces throughout Long Beach in the late 90's because of these shows. I still had never kissed anyone. I felt like a real ogre that no one ever tried or maybe I never noticed it. I always felt like Aurora's little sister, the fat chick who brings the young friends that will put up with the band's bs and while I did love the band's music, I wanted my own identity after graduating high school.

Eve and I hit it off quickly. Maybe it was my marianismo that liked befriending Blanca's older sister as a subconcious fuck you to Blanca and to my own sister. I literally never saw that awareness until I began to write this. Eve and I were both Chicano Studies majors and we both were passionate about social justice and the collective growth of our people. She was into photography and makeup. She dressed so sharp and sexy, wore way more make up than I ever cared for but it looked great on her. She had this confidence and smile that felt like someone I want to learn from and have fun with. What I am conveying here was that I looked up to her and thought only great things about her. Maybe my marianismo was dismissing red flags and being led by the ego of being wanted. Maybe my marianismo at 20 wanted to feel pretty and ladylike. I wanted some of Eve's glamour magic, the way she got ready for the night was like watching an opera singer warm up behind stage. And the energy was fun. We would watch Sex and the City and talk about our screenplay about 4 single women with magic and movement. We called it "Chicanas in the City" and we had 4 main characters that emulated different chicana paths. We loved talking about representation and creating. When we went out, I guess I felt like Carrie and she was like Samantha. She had two other friends that would hang out too, they were several years older than me and would give me makeovers and teach me about Rock en Español. While I never got used to spray on foundation, I appreciated being a part of the late night rituals.

Eve had been dating 2 guys and liked them both. She told me she had made a friend online who liked photography like her and they were going talking about photography. Days later she says he is single and I should talk to him, he agreed to talk on the phone we me. Like her sister Blanca years before, she was trying to match make me. She insisted and arranged it. His name was Angel. He was a 21 year old first gen Mexican and Boriqua college student studying photography and cinematography at Cal State Los Angeles. He was a really kind guy. He and I would talk about art, movies, Chicano studies and social justice. Talking to him felt friendly, safe and sexy. He wasn't trying to do anything or go to fast, but he was flirty and fun. By this time I had lost over 65 pounds by working out and swimming laps at the gym pool and I felt like a catch! I was waiting, hoping to be caught by someone tall, dark and artsy like him.

I remember Eve would ask me how things were going and wanted to know everything. I started feeling like she was bragging about the guys she was dating and new guys she was meeting. I was working 2 jobs and going to school, I had barely had my first kiss the year before so I was not in competition with her, that I knew. I just wanted one. One night I picked Angel up at his mom's house in South LA and I drove to Palo Verdes while Angel played me his favorite songs from this large CD book of music. The way he loved music was magnetic and deeply intimate. Meeting him in real life only a couple of times, I realize now he was a very shy artist that felt things deeply. He and I had that in common and it also got in our way. This night, though, was wonderful. We got to Palos Verdes cliffs, he showed a spot to park to enjoy the view. It was breathtaking. We sat in my car listening to Maná, Cafe Tacuba, Mazzy Star, Morissey, and more while the pacific ocean and the stars watched us. That's all we did. At the end of the evening he told me the large CD book was for me. He had spent days burning 30 CDs of what he labeled "Essential Music for Life" in black Sharpie marker. It was the first nice thing a date had ever done for me. I still have the book of cds because dang it has great music.

One night Eve texted me and said she and Angel were going to hang out that night to take photos and they wanted to stop by my work. I didn't want him to see me at work. I was a server at Luciile's BBQ and I smelled like sweat, memphis bbq, and pickles. Yet she came to the bar with him and they sat and had drinks while I finished up my shift. She offered me a ride home and I said of course, my good friend and the guy I was talking to? Duh. My best friend worked with me, she was the bar server and I was in another section. Jenn has always been protective of me and that's because she always saw me for me and didn't let anyone fuck with that. She pulled me aside and said the vibes were off with Eve and Angel that she saw Eve flirting with him and feels she is trying to make me jealous. She offered me a ride and my marianismo told Jenn she was just jealous I had a new friend and was dating because she was engaged and was always busy anyway. Clearly, I was being defensive and gave her a reminder that I wanted this.

Eve ended up driving me to her house, and this part I may never understand. She insisted I stay and watch a movie with them. That had been their plan since they were both film majors (major eye roll from me). She started drinking and I knew then I wasn't going to have a ride home as promised. The energy she used to have that felt like confidence now seemed desperate and sneaky. I hate sneaky shit. My gut will radiate until I figure out what sneaky shit you are pulling. It is my cptsd from a life of my mom lying and manipulating my feelings. It's an invisible feeling that "just knows". By this time I felt uncomfortable because I felt like they were buzzed and wanted to be alone. I could feel their chemistry and yet they were being nice to me.

Did they want a threesome? Were they going to ask me? What would I say? I hadn't even had sex with him. What is going on? Is this in my head? She is being nice but it feels nasty. Am I reading into this? Should I stay or should I go?

I stayed. I think I was in dorsal from her overpowering energy. Here's what I don't get, she told us to be in the bed, the three of us while the movie is playing. It was her by the wall, Angel in the middle and me on the edge. I turned my back on them because I felt so weird and frankly, nervous. Something was telling me they were on a date this day and I had found myself in the middle by Eve's insistence.

After about ten minutes in the dark silence, I felt the bed move next to me and Angel's body shifted from his sad to his back. Curious yet moving towards furious, I acted like I was asleep. I heard Eve whisper sexy words to him and giggling. "She's asleep now", I heard her say. She mounted Angel and they started kissing next to me. My body was ringing the alarm and I don't even know which ancestor pulled my body mass to turn to face her and while he didn't see me, she certainly did. I gave her this pissed off "Oh girl, what are you doing?" look. She giggled and buried her face onto his chest. I jumped up and insisted she take me home that moment. the first half of the ride home I was silent but by the time I knew I was almost home I let her know what I thought of her. I yelled at her and she never said anything or answered any questions. It was like I was invisible.

Later that evening Angel asked me if we were still on for our date. My marianismo yelled at him too. We ended up talking and he was way more transparent than Eve. I found out Eve had been stringing him along, too. Though she had two boyfriends, she was calling Angel weekly and flirting with him while meddling about both of us. He actually felt hurt by her, too. We decided to be friends and spent the night swapping sneaky red flags we had missed. I haven't talked to Angel in 20years and often wonder if that was even his real name but I appreciate the safety in our creative talks. Eve, on the other hand, got her friends to talk shit about me on Myspace. They were all older than me but the gaslighting they were handing me felt childish, for sure. I thought about that night for years after that. Not only did I lose the guy I liked, I lost her, the friend group and the rituals. I didn't understand it and I had to get over it, alone. Jenn was a big support when I called her crying. I was angry for years. YEARS.

Seven years later, when I was 28 and living with my now husband and stepson, Eve emailed me. She said she was in a program and needed to make amends and she took full responsibility for that night and the bullying afterwards. She asked me to forgive her and honestly, just like that, I did. But I also didn't try to be friends with her like she asked. I felt like that part of me was not available for her, her sister and their marianismo again. Their marianismo was competitive, nicenasty, manipulative and dishonest. My marianismo had been trying to impress, trying to have status, and putting the comfort of others before my own safety.

When people don't understand why someone might stay in an unsafe, disrespectful situation, consider our nervous system has gone "offline" into the highest survival strategy of Dorsal Vagal- the freeze. We as Latinas have been trained that "calladita es mas bonita" is the standard and those that tested speaking up usually faced consequences and vitriol. Much of personal and collective liberation work around healing from marianismo and machismo wounds is re-connecting back with our own intuition and body as our truth teller of what is best for us. If Eve would have apologized that same year she did those things to me I would have happily forgave her and gone back to being the 4 Chicas in the City. Thankfully, her protecters of ignoring and shaming held me then by the lesson I had to learn for myself. I had to grieve the friendship for years and every year I learned something more about my own value and how important safety is for me. It also made me realize that no one is "too good" for me to keep it real with. I had admired Eve but when the time came to choose, I learned that people don't belong on pedestals. And forgiveness is something that is done with time and sincerity. No one can force an apology, an acceptance of an apology or a promise for continued trust. That was the liberation I learned from that family. My marianismo resource now is discernment and knowing what is for me feels good for me.

My Marianismo in Relationships

I could have written this book as a bashing of machismo but I wasn't called for that assignment. This book, these spaces I have been able to share stories of marianismo with others is my divine assignment. While I can reference many books that detail how patriarchy and machismo have harmed wombholders, trans persons, and non binary persons, we could have a book club. My reason for this conversation is to address our suffering, those who feel marianismo taking over their intuition or rational mind in a way that doesn't honor their authentic needs but puts in their best protector to meditate the interaction. This is often not true connection but masking for protection. I say this as a recovering fawner, a re-imagined people pleaser, and a living ancestor of past marinistas. They have some words to share.

While marianismo has been a necessary skill of survival, it is also killing us. It has killed some of our favorite women. Whether literally or figuratively I do not take lightly the daily perpetual suffering of self identifying women. Whether they choose to stay in toxic situations or don't have a feasible way out, I feel the energy of that hurt and bear witness to so many women who are unhappy. This is to say, choose yourself, choose your body's safety and the path will become clearer with each step.

What I really want to address is the thorn that is the bitterness that unmet childhood needs creates as a protector. Have you ever met someone who is unable to receive love? Not someone who is alone and does not have love expressed to them. I am talking about someone adored by many or with a handful of close loved ones or a woman with a doting partner and they can't let the love in? This is where marianismo has left them protective, maybe bitter, maybe caustic, maybe disinterested or nonchalant, but this distance, this energy of unavailable is felt. Though I feel some sadness to admit it, I have met myself in this description. I remember one day I was so tired from staying up all night with my oldest who is a light sleeper. The next morning he wanted to be with me while I was napping and I remember yelling at him to let me rest and to close the door. The look in his eyes was like I closed the door shut on his heart, I remember instantly snapping out of it and realizing *oh no, what have I done*? This is not the kind of mess you can just clean up, this feels like pain spilling everywhere. My need for rest spilled into my son's need for security and comfort. I was unable to receive his love in that moment and shamed him for it. I would like to say that was the first and last time that has happened but that would not be true. In fact, accepting that realization and allowing myself to sit with that discomfort, I have since noticed many more times I do that. Sometimes I have difficulty sensing when I am tired and my social battery is low. I will give and give and give and then when others want me, I am resentful. It is difficult for me to accept all the love sometimes. My bandwidth of tolerance for softness was at a low and my new mom life required so much more of my receiving of love and touch, my gosh, the touch, it was so much. Since then I would say my ability to rest and receive is thriving! I remind myself of epigenetics that if I re-pair often and authentically with my children, I am activating safety and repair into their system's growth.

My Marianismo in partnerships

One day, and I remember this day well, I was feeling insecure. I was about 37 years old, a mother with two babies under 3 and a teenage stepson who adores me. And I picked an argument with Mike, my husband. "What do you like about me? I mean really, what is it? You never tell me". My husband hates when I do this because he says it is inauthentic and he shows me all the time what he loves about me when it comes up. I mean I agree, this was a low moment, for sure, and yet I still learn so much about myself and my man in that moment. His response was what it always was for me, **not good enough**. That's how my nasty marianismo comes out, a not good enough Queen of Hearts kind of sour. He said, "I like who you are as a person, how you are with people and how you make people feel. I love how you are as a mother to our kids. " And you know what I heard? "You aren't enough of anything special so I am saying these generic compliments because you're making me blah blah blah." So of course I replied with, "that's it? That's not even a thing. That's just me being me. What do you LOVE about me?" It's the next moment where I still remembering my husband healing a part of me, the 12 year old within me. He said to me with patience and a firm but not scary tone, "Cynthia, that is your inner child asking. Let me put it into words so she can understand. I love you for who you are because that is what makes you loveable. That is your gift. What you see as easy like making new friends, others feel terrified. I love how you are with people because you have a way of making people feel good and that is not the same as drawing but it is your gift". And of course, I was instantly upset that he dragged my inner child, Little Cyn into this. But also, I needed a moment to process. I saw my inner child well up with tears and her spirit walked passed us straight to the room and slammed the door, and my adult body followed. While re-parenting her, Little Cyn, in my room we both learned, acknowledged and were grateful for 3 realizations that day that continue to reveal more every year since.

1. My inner child is often projecting onto my partner what I witnessed as a child as my husband is my only other example to married life besides my parents. I saw how I often would create emotional "incidents" that I wanted him to fix and when he did I already knew it wouldn't be enough because I didn't really know what I was upset about. It was a feeling rooted in my own parent's epigenetics, not my present relationship.

2. I activate my husband's own inner child wounds when I, his partner and also the mother of his children, start raging or act cold or give confusing orders. It activates his inner child protectors and can leave him feeling unappreciated and distant. I have seen myself in a whirlwind and realized if I am reenacting something my mother has done, I wonder how this impacts him and how he felt his mother's emotions as well. I noticed he always tried to make me happy, just like his dad did with his mother. I was now hurting the boy inside him trying to uphold the home.

3. I saw my own marriage as the win I get to have. It was that day I realized my own marianismo can be toxic for me. I have cried over the realization that I could have lost this best friend of a partner because I was not fully open to receiving his love. I wanted to just give with out allowing space for his softness and protection. I saw my relationship as my legacy gift, my chance to live in the softness many many many women in my lineages did not get time or rest to do.

My Marianismo Reflections

Pulling the chicken

I filled two cups out of three cooked chicken tender sized breast pieces.
I tore the chicken- shredded it until it was puffy and transformed something small into "enough" to feed a family.
a n d   I   c r i e d   o v e r   t h e   m o u n d   o f   p o l l o
I am the pulled chicken.
I am crying that I am tired and I have no time and here I am not stopping,
pulling myself apart for everyone in my family like this shredded chicken
where the brag is how much I can expand
 how much I give and how little space I took up while giving more on the backend.
T h a t ' s   m e   p u l l i n g   m y s e l f   t o   p i e c e s   a n d   m o v i n g   o n t o   t h e   n e x t   s e l f   i n f l i c t e d   t a s k .
I am two chicken tenders but My Marianismo is a dozen crispy tacos with shredded cheese.
H a n d   p r e p a r e d   f r o m   t o r t i l l a s   t o   i c e d   w a t e r   a t   t h e   t a b l e .
There's pride and sadness about it and you only understand if you've ever been the pulled chicken.

My Marianismo Portal of Distraction

Restlessness is a distraction from the present due to past epigenetic environments
I would rather keep busy than confront either situation that feels like discomfort
Anguish is too familiar so epigenetics disassociates by being busy, full of doing, sympathetic by duty
Rest feels too close to guilt.

My Marianismo Apapachos

The word apapachar is considered one of the most beautiful words that exist.
It means "caressing with the soul". This term comes from the #Náhuatl word "papachoa", a verb used to refer to the actions of kneading, massaging or rubbing with love.

I carry more than just my dreams, I carry the inner wisdom of my ancestors and the best intentions of those that love me.

I release the the belief that I am waiting to be chosen and choose myself, everyday.

I acknowledge the child within me who had to play the part for the restless child inside my parent.

I am making space for my grief to wax and wane through me
For my grief is a memorial of my love.

I now understand those that cried so much and those that wouldn't allow themselves a tear. I hold no judgement for my ancestors and ask them for the same compassion on my journey.

I forgive myself for the era when I self abandoned. I call myself back to my own divine light.

May I honor my anger after years of fawning.
My anger is my grief protector.

It's never too late to change your mind, little one.
I don't care how "nice" they seem.
You did not arrive with less than the treasure that is naturally you.

My Marianismo apapachos

What do the parts of you feeling these words need to hear from you right now?
Like a variety of teas offered to you, help yourself and cozy up to your own soft words and warm grace.

The Leaves

My Marianismo
Epigenetic impact on The Leaves

The leaves are our capacity to expand our inner epigenetic gifts and resource them for our protection, our offering, and our JOY! Our leaves represent our ability to photosynthesize our ancestral gifts for our own expansive growth. Like photosynthesis means the process of converting sunlight into food, we can convert our epigenetic resources for creativity, intuition, skill, and magic into our own daily nourishment. Our leaves represent our ability to be in rest, joy and craft. Our leaves are our epigenetic flow when in parasympathetic mode. Our leaves hold our capacity to give and receive love and to create safety.

Leaves can look like
unlocking and unblocking your expansive potential for joy, embodying your intuition, resting for 7 lineages back and creating new cells for epigenetic joy to be photosynthesized for 7 generations forward.

Legacy Resources of our Leaves
dancing, swaying, building, singing, humming, creating, cooking resting, sewing, sowing, harvesting, communing, inspiring, loving, resting, community care

Historical trauma can impact the leaves by having a poor eco-system in which to grow. Maybe the lineage did not receive enough sunlight, food, or attention to send nutrients to the bloom. That is why the way you delight in your gifts and learn more about your inner workings is your legacy work. Creating a healthy eco-system is your part in passing along epigenetic resources of restoration and craft.

The leaves impact all chakras from the crown and third eye connection to the expression of gratitude through the throat and heart chakra, informing the solar plexus, sacral and root chakras.

"Yo no camino, yo vuelo"
-mi Tia Sara

"When we are grounding and calming our bodies, we are using our senses, borrowing from nature and the world around us. We are present with the energies surrounding us, with Earth's elements, and with our ancestors within. We are never really doing this work alone."
— Natalie Y. Gutiérrez LMFT, <u>The Pain We Carry: Healing from Complex PTSD for People of Color</u>

Being in our leaves is being a resource for our entire system from root to stem to thorns, the leaves are vital, the leaves are life and nourishment. Living in our leaves re-wires our brain to allow us to withstand developing our craft with more patience and curiosity. Our leaves have the potential to access our intergenerational highest self, the part of our consciousness that has not been limited into colonized expectations. Are leaves are our root experiences and connection to nature flowing through us. Whether out of our hands as art or back into the land as a gardener, we source our energy and either suppress it our use it for our highest good. We have more opportunity now than we may have had 3 generations back.

The hammocks and being under the trees is one way I access my ancestral connection to the land and to the lineage. It is also when I am dancing in my garden. It's also when I dance in gratitude while eating my food. I know these are my leaves because my children do it, too. She said she believes I carry gifts like her mother who traveled in her dreams and visi

My aunt says she flies in her dreams and visits beautiful places. Some call it astral projection, my aunt said her mother was known to visit people as a spirit. She would leave her human body and her spirit body would visit others to send a message or offer protection. My aunt shared she too is a dreamer who sees. "Yo no camino, yo vuelo" said my Tia Sara. She said in her dreams she flies all over seeing visions. She suggested with so much cariño I trust my visions and try my ceremony. She says she is meant to fly and spread love to others. I see myself in my dreams soaring to other realms and I wonder if I allow my leaves a bit more time in the sunshine, in the light with out interrogation or criticism of it's process, how my dreams may evolve and what other gifts my leaves hold from 14 ancestors back. A girl can dream. I am the photosynthesis of my lineage.

My Marianismo

"A matriarch is irreplaceable; that is a key component of a matriarch. Once she is gone, rarely can someone else step up and fill the hole left behind. What ends up happening is that families become aware of the void, and they try to fill it within their own family units." by Prisca Dorcas Mojica Rodriguez in *Tias and Primas*

"this work also highlights the need to return back Home: to our ancestry, to many of our practices, our medicines, our native tongues, and our communal ways of thriving, while reconfiguring and integrating these practices into the present and future."
— Jennifer Mullan, Decolonizing Therapy: Oppression, Historical Trauma, and Politicizing Your Practice

WHAT ARE LEGACY RESOURCES?

"Epigenetics proves our intuitive knowing and creative resilience as a superpower that has not only helped us survive but it is our birthright and opportunity for an expansive and joyful life. Consider that you not only carry legacy burdens but that you also have legacy resources within you waiting to help you step into your epigenetic flow and ancestral wisdom."
--Cynthia Perez, LCSW, "The ABC's Of Protecting Your Inner Child's Peace"

In Marianismo, our Legacy Resources have been conditioned through real or threatened danger of being unsafe. Our MAGIC as divine womb holders is just as complex as our indigenous dieties and their stories of misunderstanding and recreation. We too carry within us 14 generations of creativity, innovation, musicality, peaceful flow and epigenetic grace when we are in safety and connection.

As a femme you carry energy to shift the dynamic in your ecosystem for one of greed and comparison or for creating from an expansive goal with collective support. We have the ability to gather and engage with others so we must be very intentional with the power of our words and our stories we put on others or ourselves. We have so much magic that has been kept in shadows because of colonized fear, but you are the only one who knows the path for you and you are the only one who has access to your divine inner resources. When you see the inner ancestor in you, you may notice the inner ancestors in others and feel the collective shift when you and others step into your gifts as your power.

Detaching From Colonial Beliefs that limit me

Colonial expectations are gonna leave us feeling tired, depleted, maybe resentful, maybe rageful. And then it activates our epigenetics. If we're doing this now to please people to be accepted and we're doing this out of fear, survival fear that if we don't, we won't be accepted, that could be very scary. It could be life or death. Like in the beginning days of colonization. That can trigger our epigenetics.

Our cells start to open up through our epigenetics and it goes, hey, you need to fight or flight. You need to leave. This is not a good situation. Or we need to fight. We need to be snippy. We need to argue. We need to be a roadblock for this. We need to be friendly. We need to fawn. We need to say yes. We need to be a people pleaser because that is how we're going to get out of this. This is our survival.

That's when our epigenetics kind of start to go. *Hey, protection. Pssst. Ven.*
I want us to think about how when those epigenetics of our marianismo start to get unlocked because of historical trauma, how can we witness that and go, wow, this is not all mine. I was about to just go into automatic autopilot, but now I see that this is deeper than me.
How can we really balance the duality of marianismo in a way that honors our truest self?

I really have been led here by my ancestors by allowing myself to be led, but also just listening to my inner knowing, listening to my body and what feels good and what hasn't been feeling good. There was so long, I would say about 37 years of my life that I was doing things that I was taught and it still wasn't good enough. I would still be shaming myself, like self-punitive. And I realized, this isn't mine, this doesn't feel good, but yet this is my norm. And so really being able to see in my body, what doesn't feel good? And being able to pause.

I remember sitting on the bluffs in Long Beach with my good friend, Karla, whom I met in grad school. We've known each other for about 16 years now. I'm so lucky. She was telling me how she got certified as a yoga teacher. She's also a therapist and she has her own history with immigration. She told me "it's really hard to do yoga in spaces where I don't always feel safe. So I became certified in trauma informed yoga practices". She started to teach me mindfulness and I felt uncomfortable at the beginning. Once I heard Karla and the way she explained it from her perspective and her approach, my body started to soften. It made sense.

I was noticing that when I feel safe, I can receive new information. I started to see that in my meditation, whether it was me meditating with plants in movement, dancing, stomping, swaying, rocking, drumming, whether it was me reading stuff, whether it was washing my hands while I do the dishes and like really just focusing on the water, all these meditative practices were allowing me to see the colors within me, this allowed me to see what my energy truly was storing and thus projecting, and then say, whoa, that's not my energy. I have even been able to unlock times where this was not mine. I really hope this for all of us. This is just really sacred work. I really feel called in this time to share it and have more conversations around it because if we don't, who will? We also have ways within us, inner resourcing that we can use to really lead ourselves through the sacred work.

My Marianismo Legacy Resources

I hope that you can find other Marianismo resources within you because you do have them within you, inherited by you, maybe find other mother figures that can kind of reclaim that for you and really accept you as you are and then working towards that connection with your inner child to re parent them and go, you are wonderful. And I'm so sorry. I'm so sorry that your mother was limited and couldn't see this beauty in you, but I love you and I will parent you and you're exactly the child that I need. Then allowing your inner child to talk to them, the friend, to you like that. Just thinking about the beautiful resources we have and allowing ourselves to go, my gosh, I have power inherently and I am magical.

So this is an invitation. This is an invitation to your marianismo, to really look at what is mine? What is my marianismo? What do I carry inside of me? What has been passed down to me? What starts to unlock in me that is my marianismo? How have my epigenetics passed this on as a way to be a protector? And how can I let go of these things as they don't serve me now?

Can you reflect on the energy of your marianismo protectors as a burden? That's one way you can start thinking, okay, what is the energy? Is it defensive? Is it cold? Is it critical? Is it shaming? Does it feel guilty around pleasure? I would start writing it down and then ask what would you like to let go of? What would you like to walk away from with a clean slate?

And if you're like, I can't.
Whoa, what would you like to let go of? We're creating this beautiful ecosystem where you get to just float in there. What would you let go of? Imagine your pain like dropping sandbags off the side of your hot air balloon as you expand. What heavy burdens would you get rid of? I'm curious. Aren't you curious?

Lastly, what parts of your marianismo are so strong and nurturing? What ways of being do you want to protect and strengthen? Not what ways of showing up or what ways of performing or producing. What ways of just being do you want to protect and strengthen?

This is an important question because if we sit back and go, this is the lineage I was dealt, we come from a lot of trauma, there was a lot of substance abuse or violence or betrayal, I hear you and you're not wrong and I get that. But that's really allowing our life to be led by this historical trauma, this intergenerational trauma. When we reclaim it, we are actually not being this little Virgin Mary that just takes the role that she's given. We are actually decolonizing ourselves and going, "actually, I'm going to pull out my authentic self" . In that, we free the lineages seven generations back.

They're like, thank you. I've been trying to tell you, I don't want to be like this anymore. It's that I had to. And we're also just by our own energy, changing our epigenetics now, strengthening towards joy and patience and grace just by doing that. Imagine I am now an epigenetic change maker. I am now a generational healer because I'm going to show up vibrant. I'm going to show up more patient. I'm going to show up with a bigger bandwidth for tolerance.

My Marianismo Legacy Resources

An Invitation: Don't wait for your boss or people who gain something from your fawning to call out your gifts as your legacy resources. Don't even wait for your parents to come around to noticing their colonized legacy resources, go step into your calling and claim this magic that has been looking to return back to you and yours.

Maybe we could practice here with our legacy resources and saying Actually, I do have these gems and I need to first of all name it and claim it!
Label it as "My Power", "My resource", write what you are offering to your lineage as as your legacy work So thinking about it and how you walk how you show up in it
how you pull it out when it's needed, and how can you feed it more? How could you embody these resources of marianismo? Now these are just a few. I totally invite you to write your own list. Not even just a list of what your legacy resources are, but what other people who you admire, what are their legacy resources?

Connected to the elements. Notice how just getting energized with each step you take, connecting to all of the vibration of the earth, all of what the earth is telling you from here. And every step you take is just lighting you up. Then everything above you, all the wind is just protecting you.

So really when we are in our highest self, when we are allowing ourselves to process, when we are not judging or rushing, we're just being curious with our marianismo resources, we can find our intuition and our connection to the elements. When I say the elements, I mean nature, I mean the four directions, I mean earth, air, wind, and fire. We can come back to being.
I have returned to this and am a being in alignment with my intuition.

Our resourcefulness and traditions of showing love as a resource. So maybe this, maybe we were in our legacy burdens bag today. Okay. Maybe we woke up tired, too much stimulation, too many sounds and we yelled at our kids. I'm talking we as me. Okay. And then I feel bad.

And then I do that whole guilt thing and then I'm like, *I have to pull myself out of this cycle of marianismo guilt that my epigenetics likes to go on.* It likes to go, *you need to over apologize, over deliver, over sacrifice now because you had an emotion.* Can I ground myself, come back to myself as a human, as someone who also might have many human needs? Did I eat? Did I drink water? Did I explain myself? Did I move my body? What do I need? But I can come back with my resourcefulness and my traditions of showing love, right? Once I am grounded in this resource myself, I can be abundant with it. This is my epigenetic flow.

I can prepare a beautiful meal for my children. I can sit with them and say, "hey, I don't like the way this energy was in my body. It didn't feel good to say that to you. And I'm still feeling it. So I can imagine you are too. And I'm really sorry. That's not my intention and can you forgive me?" I'm able to shift my traditions, whether I receive that or not, I'm able to go, *this is the tradition, because I am the mother and I am really standing in this.*

Unburdening my marianismo with awareness and compassion, what does that look like?

Welcoming my marianismo with grace and finesse, what does that look like?

Celebrating our successes and our togetherness with safe masculinity and the energy of collective love is described in this song that highlights the elders with compassion and the new generation as a voice of expansive liberation. This song is a gift to the collective.

Lyrics for <u>Cumbia de mi Barrio</u> by Las Cafeteras

Somos de la tierra, somos de maíz
Mire como baila la gente aquí
Cuando el biri-biri mueve nada me duele
El bom-bom que me pege levanta la plebe
Mira mi abuela
Viene con su chela
Y no puede parar
Cuando el ritmo pega ni puede rezar
Gozando la cumbia de frente, para atrás
Las doñas de mi barrio hasta el sur de Panamá
Sur de Panamá
Vamos todos a bailar
Pa' sentirnos bien
Ah-ah-ah
Vamos todos a gozar
Todo va estar bien
Ah-ah-ah
Desde Africa hasta Belize
Paris a Bangkok, la raza muy sexy
La mezcla en el baile me pone muy feliz
Esta cumbia de mi sangre y lo traje para ti
Lo traje para ti
Lo tra-, tra-, tra-, tra-, traje para ti
Nacimos de mujeres
Nacimos de las flores
Y no tengo país
Crezco donde quiera, mira la raíz
El ritmo de mi pueblo suena muy feliz
Es la cumbia de mi barrio y lo canto para ti
Lo canto para ti, ti, ti, ti, ti
Vamos todos a bailar
Pa' sentirnos bien
ah-ah-ah (ah-ah-ah)
Vamos todos a gozar
Todo va estar bien

My Marianismo

Timeless — Breaking Cycles

WHAT ARE THE LEGACY RESOURCES OF MARIANISMO?

- shapeshifting capabilities come in clutch
- resourceful and creative with what is around and can whip up magic como si nada
- grassroots energy and collective protectiveness by looking out for others and passing on vital information
- crisis management skills are rooted in ancestral wisdom
- can transmute pain into craft and create abundance
- the ability to pivot and read the room for safety
- our intuition and indigenous connection to the elements.
- our resourcefulness and traditions of showing love as a resource
- celebration holders, ceremony makers, ritual mentors
- We are portals to above and below and within

Dancing
Stomping
Singing
Swaying
Touch
Crafting
Tinkering
Meandering
Wandering
Humming
Floating
Laughing
Crying
Eating
Hosting
Grounding
Weaving
Storytelling

What are your legacy resources?

What are your lineages' legacy resources?

What did they do in joy and rest?

What were they exceptional at?

Writing Invitations:
1. Write a letter to your ancestors acknowledging and inviting their legacy resources
2. Make a list of the lands your ancestors are from and doodle in the plants, fruits, animals and customs

Living in our Legacy Resources

Maybe you want to see how you would embody those resources. One of them is shape **shifting capabilities, being able to read the room**. Because we've had the legacy burden of having to serve everybody, of having to connect people by gathering, we've become really good at shape shifting our roles. We go from server to cook to nanny to housekeeper to businesswoman to bill payer.
We are really exceptional at shape shifting. So always remember that it's gonna come in clutch for you. It's gonna come in clutch in survival and what if we are also the phoenix that shapeshifts the fire into a body of energy that soars through past pain with energized purpose and clarity? So lean into that when you're feeling a burden. How can I shape shift right now for myself, for my spirit, for my inner child? What if the noticing of the burden in your body is the first reminder that you may need to level up, to get boundaried, to shape shift into the divine purpose that seeks you?

Resourceful and creative with what is around and can whip up magic como si nada. Okay, so we are able to be resourceful in a very literal and figurative way we go "Okay, I got some yarn. I got some leaves, you know bundle that up and we got a ceremony". I'm gonna make up a fire because I know how to do that, we know how to use what we have and work with it to shift the energy. This is a really big deal; please don't minimize this magic.

I noticed that when I was thinking about it in this way, I felt some kind of guilt. I go, my gosh, if I can do that, if I could use what's around me and change the energy for good, it helped me see the burden that I cause when I am in my low vibrational marianismo. When I am in bad energy and I snap at my kids without walking away to check myself or to take a nap, now I'm also projecting that powerful energy onto them. If it's bad energy, that's still sticking with them. That's like putting my susto onto them. That is how powerful my energy is. So I want to be really, really intentional, present and creative with the resource that is my own life force energy.

Living in our Legacy Resources

When I resource my creative energy, I want to make sure that it's in goodness. I want to whip it up; como si nada, but in a beautiful flow- grassroots energy and collective protectiveness by looking out for others and passing on vital information in real time. We're really good at keeping the tea hot. we know the scoop and yet don't run to share it with everyone. We are protectors of stories. We're good at keeping time still, holding space for our comadres, our community, being a safe place for people to go. And we're also good at sharing what needs to be shared with discernment. When we're in our highest self with discernment to protect people, we are in our legacy gifts. Thinking about in our lineage, *who were those people that said, no, I don't care if I'm the black sheep, I stand in my values.*

This is the truth and I'm going to speak it.
We have within us these grassroots energy that is an advocate, that is a truth teller, and we can harness that and we could pass on this vital information for others.
We have crisis management skills that are rooted in ancestral wisdom. When we're like, my gosh, I know what to do. I feel like I need to drum. I need to dance. I need to go for a run. I need to jump in the ocean. Consider yourself a living ancestor connected to your instincts.

" I don't know why I just have to I feel like I'm losing my mind. I need to cut my hair". Consider that that might be your ancestral wisdom again those epigenetics going "What's going on?" and our ancestors are like *I got this* and then it starts to percolate it starts to do its business like coffee ready, steam piping hot out the top like, *I know what to do*.... consider that we have these beautiful resources that get us out of things.

Glamour Magic is our ability to empower ourselves with our own inherent magic of our beauty, our confidence, our essence. Unlike materialism which is shallow performance of obtaining things for status, our glamour magic is shifting energy from stigma to enchantment. While marianismo has gender roles that can be burdens, imagine when you show up full in your beauty in your own standards of what beauty you share, it is shifting your self confidence from dorsal vagal to calm and in parasympathetic. While I can hear my mom telling me to add earrings or put on red lipstick before leaving, that is her way of sharing lineage secrets of being in our glamour magic to be seen and heard. When we use our glamour magic of dressing in a way that shows our creative spirit, our professionalism, or our non-binary beauty, we start to move in a way that showcases our light, we start to soften our petals and open up towards the sun because we feel good, we feel magical, we sparkle. From the stigma that red lipstick is for putas, to wearing it as reclaiming the power red lipstick holds for all faces and the science behind red being protection over what we say and the attraction that our lips cause others to hear what we are saying. Distracted by our beauty and enchanted by our essence, we got what we need, thanks to our legacy resource of glamour magic.

Season 2 episode 8 "Money, Marianismo, and Magic" with guest Jai Correa, The Matriarch Healer and Season 3 Episode 3 "Queer Magic" with guest Luis Cornejo, LMFT is a companion episode for this energy.

Living in our Legacy Resources

We can pivot the room for safety. Created out of the need to survive, sure, but sharpened the ability to move ahead by noticing nuances, eye contact, a subtle brow raise or the rise in the neighbor's paranoia of your success, we are skilled by burden, at reading the room. Maybe we feel intimidated in some rooms because we can sense their biases or our epigenetics of past caste trauma tells us "this ain't for us" and we feel a tingle down our spine. We can read the room for social sustainability, quickly stepping into our people pleasing ready to help persona. What if we created our own rooms and everyone was safe to be visible and authentic? Imagine our Marianismo abundantly resourceful and generous in the room? That's a beacon of hope and love.

We are loving resources. We have been told that spanking our children or "la chancla" is how were raised obedient hard working children. And while that may appear to be the result, when we spank or make our children fear us, they are obedient only because we have moved them into a "dorsal vagal" response of their autonomic nervous system. This is not the flex we have been sold. When we have our own children in dorsal vagal, not only is this not good for their physical health because it slows down their heart rate and sends a message to their brain that they are in a life or death situation, this breaks their spirit. That is NOT who our people are. That is what religion has pitted us up against, a last option of "be quiet or I will scare your body so much your soul leaves and your body will do what I demand it to" and we have made that reaction part of our lineage "inheritance" as a way of surviving oppression and harsh labor.

Remember, we can advocate for the collective even when others call it "complaining". We come from the earth and the stars, we are capable of expansive LOVE and grace just like the cosmos we come from. When you imagine your expansive love, if it feels like you weren't given many examples, go be a child of the sun, the water, the moon, the wind. Allow the many energies of the earth to parent and re-parent you. Let the sand kiss your feet as you run straight towards the waves and remember the child within you as your body squeals with delight at the cold shock of water's touch. Find your loving resources by witnessing yourself through the reflection of how gentle you are with squirrels or geese at your local park. Stop yourself from your busy day and let the sunshine warm your inner glow. Cry to the moon and let her brilliance beam down through your crown to remember your ancestor's love and wishes for you to be gentle, slow, and beloved to the lineage of humans and animals you come across.

We are the ceremony holders, the tradition and the ritual. How do we want to teach the next 7 generations? How do we honor the divine time we have on this land? How are you reclaiming your power everyday? This is a call to take up space, to create space and to honor space as it trusts you to hold it, with sacred grace, radical advocacy and intimate transparency to those who are open to this legacy.

The Stem

My Marianismo
Epigenetic impact on The Stem

The Stem has the transformation potential. This is where we can pass up our legacy resources and our legacy burdens.
The stem represents the body, the spine, the autonomic nervous system. The body reacts via messages sent by the roots (epigenetics) or the bloom (mind). The stem is where we can communicate new ways of showing up, of detaching, and of allowing new neural pathways to form.

The stem is the switchboard to survival or restoration. The stem is protected by the leaves and the thorns and can choose to lean on the legacy burdens and resources they offer as nourishment or protection.

Stem highways holds space for:
epigenetic flow, epigenetic freeze, epigenetic flight, changemaker, shapeshifting, code switching, new neural pathways

Stem work impacts the body and physical dis-ease and illness in the body and can change epigenetics for joy and expansiveness

Historical trauma can have the stem in fight/flight or dorsal mode as a way of surviving religious indoctorination, exploitation and enslavement.

This impacts the Solar Plexus chakra. This informs a Ser vs Susto response on the epigenetic highway.

In *Decolonizing Trauma Work Indigenous Stories and Strategies*, author Renee Linklater, a member of Rainy River First Nations in the traditional territory of Treaty #3 shared this story of her experience in a home swing as what is pictured as "swing therapy" with an elder named Darlene whom she was interviewing on her healing methods. "After we smudged, Darlene told me that she would like to show me what she does, that she would like me to go in the swing. I welcomed her suggestions. I lay down on the swing and closed my eyes. She sang songs and swung me. She sang songs and swung me. I returned to a time when I was a little baby. It was very comforting, I felt very warm and safe. While in the swing my mother came to visit me. I could see her kneeling down beside the swing, holding the edge with her hands and looking in to me with thoughtfulness and love. My heart started to race. I felt the fear of separation, of abandonment and the fear of being unprotected. When it was time to come out of the swing, Darlene shared with me that she felt that I was afraid. She prayed that I would be provided with what I needed to do this work; she prayed for courage, bravery and strength." (Linklater, R, 2016).

When I read this passaged I closed my eyes and gave thanks, to the author, to Darlene, and to my Tia Sara and her mother. My maternal grandmother weaved hamacas, that I knew. But the truth is I didn't appreciate the effort or the craft, I just enjoyed the spoils of the swing. I can't say I didn't always honor the hamaca because I have. Whenever anyone goes back to the motherland I request an hamaca or an huipil. I didn't think more of the penchant for those requests other than the nostalgia of Mexico in those two items for me. Fast forward I am a 35 year old mother of 3 and over the years I have saved 4 hamacas. I went to Merida with my mother and son in 2022 and again in 2023 and my aunt gifted me an hamaca each time. There I was in my garage trying to hide 6 hamacas from my husband. As I held these hamacas and refolded them with delicate care, I started to think about the magic they hold. They memories they create space for. The colors they are made with as an intention, a protection. I started to feel with this hamaca. Some may say I started to reawaken.

Tia Sara has always been a loving energy to me. She is not only one of my favorite cooks in the world, she has the heart of her mother and a fire for all the women before her. She will make you a meal, tend to your tears and give you the truth. She is a safety for me. And in many ways, she stands in for a grandmother I did not get to know well because of separation due to immigration. I called my Tia Sara months after our latest trip to Merida with her and I told her about my dreams that wouldn't stop visiting me. I shared with her in my dreams I saw a beach with my hamacas and I was smudging someone and the hamacas. I told her I saw myself so beautifully as I walked someone to the hamaca and led them into a hammock ceremony. I saw all the details of the ceremony. This first dream had only one hamaca and it was a clear vision, almost a directive.

I felt this pull to offer this as a healing medicine, but had my doubts. Who am I to do this? I am not from Yucatan, I live here. My Tia became tearful with pride and said she believes she was sent by her mother to gift me these hamacas and encourage me to do what I saw in my dreams. She said I should ask my abuela for guidance and trust the rest to happen. I have sense held private, intergenerational mother and daughter, and small group hammock ceremonies under the trees and on the land. That is me in my stem, in my epigenetic flow. I am not just the ancestor of a hammock laborer, it is a craft, it is a medicine, it is an offering of love from my lineage to yours. Being on the land activates my roots which awakens my stem. My stem sends up whatever nutrients I am offering it and when I accept that my medicina is something I may not have been taught in school and that it is actually quite powerful intuitively, I soar. I connect with the animals on the land and I swear the squirrels are on their best behavior for us all the way through. the geese often make a grand appearance, they tend to be gregarious. The participant, they come as an aligned calling, too. I have always received the person I am meant to hold space with because it is felt from the fist call. This is my stem magic. This is unlocking all those hours crafting this colorful nest that is a swing and a home to babies and elders alike.

Detaching from root fears can be noticing what burdens you're carrying, acknowledging them. Are these yours or have they been sourced through the root from a place of ancestor's fear? We are not powerless, we can be a witness and then cutting the energetic cords of attachment to allow for new healthy roots to form.

In my stem life I am currently more mindful of what I am passing on to my children and if they choose to have children, what memories their bodies hold. I have abundant ideas about holding space for Marianismo platicas and working with the youth to learn about the science of their fascinating living ancestor, their bodies! I as a stem am a changemaker, a love energy that moves from my roots to my crown with fluidity when in rest. I can become change and tradition. It is within me because it came from me.

With a hand on your heart and one on your tummy, standing tall like a tall rose bush, if you feel called, take a deep slow inhale imagining the color of the energy you are calling into your body and let it swirl in your root/tummy. Imagining your hope for your self, slowly exhale, exagerate the slowness if you can, and exhale gratitude to this stem, this communicator of everything going on around you, the protector of your systems, the only body you have. Deep exhale and gratitude for our stem.

Creating new neuropathways for joy and intuition through the stem

Taking information from the leaves, like photosynthesis to our divine stem as new neuropathways, new ways of being fully in our spirit and bodies with our intuition sourced and our clarity safe.

"I don't know why I just have to I feel like I'm losing my mind. I need to cut my hair"

What if..... you consider that that might be your ancestral wisdom again, those epigenetics going " "What's going on?"

 And our ancestors are like I got this and then it starts to percolate, it starts to do its business like coffee ready to come smoking out the top like "I know what to do".

 Consider that we have these beautiful resources that get us out of things.

The other thing is we can transmute pain.

Ooh, our epigenetics passes on, sure, it passes on pain, but it also goes, I know what we did with this pain. And our epigenetic sends the cellular memory, the cellular code. I think of it like Morse code, like beep, beep, beep, boop, boop, boop, boop. And then we act out, right? So imagine we can transmute this pain into craft and create abundance from it.
We do it all the time. We are so creative. When you like think about when you seen a woman say, I don't know how I'm gonna get these kids feds, but she gets it, right? She creates this meal out of her pantry. She comes up with a new way to sell something or she makes up a beautiful piece of art after a divorce, after child loss. She is transmuting that pain into abundance, into craft, into artistry.

And that is her way of passing it through. So remembering that our creativity is so important, so important as a legacy resource and the way we process could very well be through movement, dance, emotion, art.

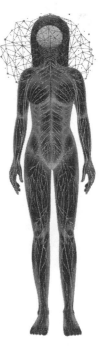

The epigentic flow of My Marianismo

So just like a plant has photosynthesis and plant cells that send the nutrients, the energy to different parts of the plant as it needs it, I invite you to think about yourself as a plant starting at the roots, who I have always been or who my ancestors, with the DNA that they gave me in my brain stem that carries seven generations on each side.
This root is now activated and it's going to guide me.
I have legacy resources and these are our leaves, right?
These leaves recieve the sun. These are like, ooh, remind me sun energy of all the goodness that I am. These are our gifts that are remembered, unlocked. The leaves hold our magic.

My ability to be in flow, my connection to water, my rhythm and movement, my ability to gather people, my softness with my children when acting from my love source, that's my epigenetic flow. My prana energy, my life force energy.

This is how I get into my parasympathetic. I know it. My resource, my epigenetic resource is trying to say, *hey, do this, these things and you'll feel better*. It gets me to parasympathetic, which is calm, which is confident and able to handle the situation. Think about if we're a rose, we also got those thorns. What do thorns do? They're protecting, right? They protect, they take up space on the stem and demand to be felt. They are impactful.

The rose that is still growing, that rose has a job to do, which is to bud, to create more abundance and fragrance. To let bees pollinate and then the bees go do their thing. They're part of an ecosystem and the thorns are part of it to protect the mission.
When thinking about our thorns as another epigenetic gift that we have inherited (subconsiously counts) gotten from our ancestors in the form of our DNA, in the form of our epigenetics. These can now be more like thorns. I'm not saying that these are bad. I said that these are thorns. But these could also look like the legacy burdens we have to carry. How I have to act, how quiet I have to be, how I have to be productive, how I feel guilty being in rest, right? How guilty I feel. This gets me quickly into a sympathetic or dorsal mode. I got to fight or flight now. I got to freeze. I can't speak.
This is a thorn trying to protect me, trying to like throw me some nutrients to a situation that helped in the past. It's not good or bad. It was something that an ancestor's DNA knows as a survival from these root feelings. I don't want to feel this.
Do these thorns protect our cells, protect this discomfort? Do they numb us to be cold and closed?

I can thank these protectors. "Thank you for the way that you avoided that because I know that you feared it." And also if it's not serving me, teasing it out and going, "I see that this is something I needed to react in, but this isn't serving me and I don't need to carry this moving forward." And just noticing when the thorns show up for you, when the protectors go, no, no, no, no, no, don't do that.

When we are in our epigenetic flow we are activating our truest self, our authenticity. When we are ritually in our flow we are not only re-wiring our brain to create new neural pathways for joy, we are also expanding our bandwith of tolerance to handle sudden changes, crisis and strengthening our inner trust to be able to pivot in new transitions. This is what we grow for future generations and relish in now.

Asking now, is that a rational thought that I'm having or is this is this a response from my root fear? Is this rooted from my historically colonized body? What sends the message of how it's going to be on our nervous system and our capacity from day to day, moment to moment? So if we've had a day where we're overstimulated, we had our supervisor make us feel worse, we are short on time, we haven't had rest, we haven't had a good meal we're probably going to lean into our thorns. If we allow ourselves to go on a walk, take a nap, limit the people that make us feel triggered or overactive, then maybe we have time to let the sun hit our leaves, our legacy resources we can then recreate. Imagine yourself detaching from the idea that they're "good or bad". It's just where am I acting from now? The roots? The Thorns? The leaves? And mind you, thorns come in handy for protection when needed. It's just that we don't want to be all thorns, right? If we cut off all the leaves, it wouldn't get any sunshine and it wouldn't be able to, you know, do the photosynthesis.

If we didn't have the thorns, the beautiful stem wouldn't be protected. It gives it the firmness, right? The structure. So it's a balance, that duality of marianismo. And then what sends the energy or the information or the action of what we're doing? Well, this is polyvagal toning. This is our vagus nerve. This is the stem.
The stem, that is our **epigenetic power** to shift our behavior into new expansive beliefs. I say this is what makes you a changemaker going,

Whoa, I almost got caught up in my thorns. Let me take a moment. Let me go dance to my favorite song. Let me go cry. Let me go take a shower. Let me go yell into a hole and pass up different epigenetic switches that are going off in my body. This is where I can change the course. This is my epigenetic flow. I'm gonna transmute how I wanna go and hurt something into something beautiful and grounded and truly me.

I'm gonna use this anger and rage and I'm gonna stomp it out to some drums. I'm going to draw it out and now I'm in my epigenetic flow. Now I'm reaching a different part of my ancestral magic and I might physically feel in flow. I might feel an energetic flow where I feel lighter. I feel like I am almost carried. I feel like a buzz around me. I might feel in my epigenetic flow with the elements where nature is talking to me.

And I'm feeling like I'm just, you know, as if being put back together by the wind and the trees and the soil beneath me.

So **epigenetic flow** is when your epigenetics are aligned with your present energy body and spirtual activation. Epigenetic flow is specific to you and what that feels like. Maybe you're dancing while cooking and you're singing a song while cooking and your food comes out delicioso, so good. And you're like, why? I actually didn't even have all the ingredients. It's you! You put that epigenetic flow in. You were the change maker that made that food delicious.

Do you see? It's your sazon. We can allow ourselves to bring up the epigenetic change that we wanna be, and then we get to see our blossom, our beautiful rosebud.

I wanna remind you about the rose. Have you seen a rose at night? Have you seen it early in the morning? It closes up. It knows what to do. It knows when to protect itself naturally. It can still be soft, but it still has the memory of those thorns saying, hey, now's not the time. It's dark and cold out here. And it can still close up.
But when the sun's out and it feels safe, because safety is the key, right? It expands and it blossoms and it shows you all its colors, its beautiful layers of petals, right? It welcomes animals to it. It has a scent, a fragrance. It has this zesty color, just all its own. The rose may even have like a funky name, a cool, funny name to remember.

So what are our petals? Our petals are us, how we show up.
All of this work from the roots to my bloom, how it looks to others. This looks like me in my Marianismo magic, my bloom. I've blossomed into who I wanna be. I'm showing you my petals, but this looks like blooming. This looks like abundance, meaning I have multiple streams of joy. I am picking up different hobbies, I'm trying different things for myself. I am not guilting myself. I'm allowing abundance. I'm allowing abundance of people helping me, receiving care, asking for assistance. I am in my essence. People might say I'm glowing because I'm in my divine essence. I'm really just showing people the way I do things without worrying about their approval because I delight in myself. And then I have my intuition on 10.

My intuition is telling me who I am, how I can show up and it's unlocking more within me and I'm trusting it. I'm letting it guide me so then it's an open channel, an open portal this is also going to give me softness. If you ever feel like you don't know how to be soft because you weren't raised in softness but you can unlock softness from maybe memories that you've blocked or even ancestral memories of softness in your lineage in different ways.

When you start to feel yourself being in your own softness, you alone get the joy of going *my gosh, this is me. This is actually who I am. I am capable of softening*. It's gonna feel so beautiful because it's of your own making.

You did it! It can feel like you are the embodiment as your own lineage change maker. I know it's possible because we all started as divine inner children that were just full of honey and joy and purity and it was dampened, but we can get back to that.

Doing things with love as the medicina of marianismo

My paternal grandmother is Raquel Espinoza Alonzo and she is a big part of the behind the scenes of this journey. She is the mother of my father and my tia Sara and my late tio Carlos. Her husband, my grandfather, was Manuel Alonzo, the oldest of 5 siblings. My abuelos were humble people with a profound story if you ask for the cosmology of it. They have a legacy that is still being lived through me and my cousins and siblings. When I am in my deepest awareness I can feel them in the field of my conscience, the portal to maya cosmovision, I like to imagine.

One thing I always heard about my dad's parents was "fueron muy pobres, indios del pueblo" which is a very caste system way to talk about a person and Merida being the first region colonized by Diego De Landa makes where my family comes from, heavy on the heirarchies. What I am trying to say is they were looked at as merely poor people from los pueblos that were laborers. But that is not all they were and yet, hiding in plain sight was also part of their magic.

There are many incredible stories of magic, curanderismo, santeria, and fantasmas in our lineage that are for the right time and the right listener as these are sacred stories. But what I do want to share I feel they would be in agreement with as my intention is love and elevation.

This side of my lineage also comes from a historically significant land. I recently discovered my grandfather's birthplace is Chicxulub, Mexico, 30minutes from Merida and located on a beach. The fascinating thing is the impact of an asteroid 66.0 million years ago on what is now the Yucatán Peninsula of Mexico at Chicxulub which caused the extinction of 75% of life on Earth, including non-avian dinosaurs, and marine reptiles. This crash created cenotes that not only served as the main source of water for the Maya, it also became a vital part of the ecosystem and a sacred place connecting the Maya to the underworld. My connection with my grandfather and the underworld has been part of my own marianismo healing. I had always wondered more about Maya culture and felt disconnected when schools referenced European history as the vital history and Maya inventions were a footnote of a forgotten people. This has been a way to diminish the magic of the land & people.

On *Confetti All Around* Season 2 episodes 14 & 15 I talk with Vero, Denise and Amparo about a family constellation ceremony Vero held and we all were there as witness and participant. In this constellation my abuelo Manuel came through with anger and an opportunity for me to see him for his gifts as well. You see, my grandfather completed suicide by hanging, something he had been fascinated with since he was young. What has been a family wound has revealed for me layers of ancestral attachment wounds and the roles of women in this pain. In a family constellation, it was witnessed that my paternal grandfather Manuel was sexually, emotionally and physically abused by his mother. This would change the energy in his Spirit. He and his sons and his grandsons all have a speech impediment, a stutter when they are anxious or have a lot on their mind. The females do not appear to have this stutter but we inherited this energy to care for partners and brothers because we can feel their pain in an extreme empathy due to the need to protect. This abuse by his mother left him feeling a lack of safety, of love and he was unable to receive love from his family. He used jokes to project his pain. This abuse changed his epigenetics.

Doing things with love as the medicina of marianismo

If given ample love and support of his gifts, who could my grandfather have been for our lineage?

What his mother must have been raised with limited the love my grandfather received and that lack, that longing, that sacred anger for his dreams unlived manifested into his descendants.

My grandfather had a 2nd grade education because he was the caregiver of his 5 siblings. As the oldest child his parents often left town and put Manuel in charge of the kids without money or food. My grandfather longed for affection form his parents and gave more attention than he was given. He was an exceptional reader and researcher. He was his own teacher and taught his siblings through stories, chistes and music. He guides my writing through bibliomancy and when I am in my epigenetic flow, I know he sends me the research or the people to collaborate with to create my work. I know this work is part of his potential and I am honored to carry this manuscript past the finish line for him, for us.

My grandfather's machismo was what my father calls an "ignorant mysoginist" and what my tia said was selfish and cruel. Being a "lightskinned Mestizo with green eyes" he often ridiculed my grandmother Raquel throughout their marriage. This made all of her children angry that he always teased her while she did everything for her children. I see now that he took out on his wife the sacred rage he held for his own mother and this wound bled onto his family.

My grandfather Manuel completed suicide years after my grandmother died. I believe it was her love that kept him alive way past what he desired for himself. He was always "obsessed" with the macabre, with death and with nooses. Once my grandmother passed it was like his spirit was lost without the loving care my grandmother gave him. She never abandoned him even when he was doing so many things that would ask a partner to leave, my grandmother in her marianismo would cry about my grandfather's lack of help and disabling behavior. Yet, she acknowledged his pain in a way that was helping our lineage's karma and epigenetics now. She was giving us balance, order and cariño by what she gave to her own family.

Doing things with love as the medicina of marianismo

My Tia Sara is the story teller for me to reconnect with my grandmother's essence. My Tia Sara says my grandmother always said you should do things for others with love or don't do it at all. If you are doing it with resentment than say no, set the boundary, and move on. If you're doing it out of kindness and love, then show it, "do all things with love." That phrase has been one that snaps me back into my intention to be grace for my children, to be present with their curiousity and cariño. The irony is not lost on me that I went to college twice to earn degrees to do therapy only to now be interested in indigenous healing and rites of passage. My abuela is a woman who was always practicing with her plantitas, florida water, and her cleansing rituals. The other day my 72year old father was over and we were about to take care of family business that had been weighing heavily on us. Before leaving my house I asked my dad if I could do some energy healing with him. He said with a calm heart, "Sure Flo, I trust you." I applied agua de florida on him with my hands and held his face. He inhaled deeply and asked what the scented water was. After I told him he got teary eyed and stated "my mom used to put that on us everyday before we left the house for school, just like you did. I had forgotten that and the smell just now reminded me of those moments." That memory meant so much to me. I felt as if my grandmother was applying the refreshing agua and holding her son's face through me and it felt like an honor.

Meditation and indigenous spiritual rituals is one way I have reclaimed for the parts of me that did not feel "Mexican enough" or "Yucatecan" or even deserving of connection with grandparent ancestors that did not know me because I only visited a few times while they were alive. I had this moment with a message and a warm and peaceful feeling of love come over me in a meditation with my Abuela Raquel in which I asked her how I get to know my lineage if they didn't know me and I haven't lived in Mexico. Ancestors replied, "We longed to know you and though borders and time kept us apart, in this realm there are no borders and no time, we are available to know you now". I felt this ease in my day accepting that I am in fact so loved that while I may have felt alone as a child of immigrants, I was wondering whom I came from and my lineage too was longing to learn who came from them, too.

I remember when I received my first chakra reading at a "Goddess Retreat" my cousin Alyssa had invited me to. I was skeptical but the one person I connected with was a chakra reader whom I signed up with. She had me lie down with my eyes closed while she guided me into a meditation she was swinging a crystal pendulum up and down over my body, over my energy fields. She was writing stuff down like she said she would. What was going on in my consciousness was it's own unlocking. One feeling I instantly felt was resistance to allow this woman to completely be in my unconscious mind too long and moving things around. I suddenly got distracted and swept up into this portal of relaxation where I found myself in the living room of Raquel and Manuel Alonzo. I know because I had visited their home in Merida before as a child and teenager and remembered so many details in this field of consciousness. I felt like my grandmother's guest of honor. I walked instinctively to her bedroom. She had a small home so it wasn't much difficulty to see the space. As I looked into her bedroom my body felt light and every step felt so real. I saw on her wall the same print of La Angel de la Guardia walking the two children home over a broken rope bridge with a hologram rainbow in the distance. That print is what really made me know I was in her room. Then I looked at the bed and it was me in her bed, It was me in her role but as myself. It almost felt like an initiation, nothing scary about it, more like this passing of a knowing.

Doing things with love as the medicina of marianismo

Since that day, I have found my way back to that living room, the bedroom, even my grandmother's kitchen and backyard to consult with the matriarch of the home when I needed to meet her on her turf. I can close my eyes and beam myself into this loving space and meander through getting to know her more. I see her sewing machine in the kitchen corner. I see eggs on the counter from her chickens. I see how she made her own remedios and had her own rituals for her joy. I meet her here when I feel alone or need some courage. She has never not shown up whether it is a feeling, a message or a memory, I have been able to feel her give love in a way that I can take it with me.

I have replayed moments I have been connecting with my abuela Raquel through epigenetics often without even realizing it. The obvious connections would be that I love wearing huipiles where some people may look down on it. I host hammock homecomings on the land and I believe my grandmother's craft and healing remedios are passed down to me through her guidance in those intimate moments with those called. The last story I will leave you with is one I still feel in my lungs. My father always says wonderful things about his mom and also shares that she had a hard and sad life being very poor and always having to be the responsible parent while his father drank the money away. My grandmother would be at her sewing machine producing products to feed her children. She cried a lot, they said.

One day when I was seven months pregnant with my first full term pregnancy, I got a wild, no, not wild, intuitive, an instinctual idea to sign up for a sewing class with my local parks and rec. I had always wanted to learn how to sew and that period in my third trimester seemed like the perfect time. I signed myself up for the beginner apron making six week class. The day of the class I was on edge and anxious about my high risk pregnancy. I remember picking a fight with Mike and heading to class early to calm down. I waddled into the fabric store where the class was being held and I started to feel things. I felt calm, I felt inquisitive, I felt, eager. They told us to pick out fabric for our apron. I found myself feeling the textures and smelling the samples. I felt sentimental. I couldn't make sense of it because I didn't have any prior connections to sewing. I brushed the deep feelings off as shame and nerves. When the class started the teacher was an older lady and she was so kind and patient. Feeling very pregnant I found myself having a hard time paying attention, when it was time to start our projects I started worrying about the argument with Mike and I felt behind in the apron. I just burst into tears in front of the sewing machine in class. I just couldn't stop. I asked the teacher if I could leave my apron and start again next week and she said of course. The other participants gave me some pregnancy support about how pregnancies bring waves of feelings and I thanked them. I sat in my car and sobbed. I couldn't breathe, I felt so much sadness and grief. I felt a longing. I felt something was missing and I was feeling the impact of that loss. That day was nine years ago and now I truly believe, given everything I know about epigenetics and ancestral technology, I believe I was crying as a connection to my grandmother's epigenetics. I imagine she cried often while very pregnant with each of her 3 babies and sewing at all hours for survival. I realize now she was the call I felt to learn how to sew, like a protective plan to always be able to provide for myself. Like nesting in preparation for baby. Like bilateral stimulation and rhythmic flow through machine and craft. Maybe I was trying to be closer to her and we both cried that day in the fabric store. She got me there, she picked out the fabric, and we cried at the weaving of our motherhood stories. What a loving and intentional act she did and I tried. I think I will try again.

La Buena Suerte

Some of my most shameful moments as a step mom and a biological mom have been when I am acting from my low vibrational marianismo. When I am tired and insist on cleaning on Sunday morning whle raging on my family about how no one helps me, my marianismo has been looking for attention. I have learned through listening to my body that my marianismo is seeking time with myself, not with others and not helping others. When I feel resentful it is probably a deeper projection that I feel I self abandoned by not setting limits in the first place. I am working on being actively curious about my resentment. I want to give it grace and follow it around to how it got here. Another quality I have witnessed in myself is difficulty staying in rest in the present. I say we will watch a movie together then after ten minutes into the movie I am offering to make my kids snacks and then I end up cleaning the kitchen and leaving my kids to watch the movie alone, again. This is my usual script. I have more trauma information about my lineage now to understand my own restlessness which has roots from my great grandmother who suffered the deaths of two children, her spouse and the disappearance of her oldest son for three years. When I put all the pieces together I felt her, pacing, cleaning, searching, moving around to make the anguish manageable. I could feel the numbness needed by the body to make the ache of this sacred grief not take a mother out.

La Buena Suerte was the name of a tienda my mother's maternal grandparents owned and operated in Mexico. My mom mentions the shop with great nostalgia. She describes walking into her grandparents shops seeing large glass candy jars by the register and they let her fill a bag with loose candies of her choosing. I saw myself feel pride for my past ancestors' accomplishments and in that moment I realized they too must feel pride for mine. And if they had this entrepreneurial spirit, then maybe I did, too. It make me start to make time to call in the gifts that were within me. I noticed some of my proudest marianismo moments are when I am in my bag, baby. In my marianismo epigenetic flow I am in parasympathetic, I am calling in my ancestral remembering, I am the self ceremony, I am adding on to their gifts and sharing with my children. I have witnessed myself make my kids costumes out of random household objects, fix up a delicious pantry meal out of what's in the cupboards and have these kids asking for seconds. I have witnessed how when I take the moment to dance with my youngest, our energies link up and spread happy dust throughout the room like a disco ball. I noticed when I give my first born back rubs with the right firmness he likes, he starts chatting about his goals and gratitudes, so much so that I think I have found my magic calming spell. I have noticed that when I make my oldest son a cup of hot tea, he will usually stay in the living room to drink it which gives us eager family members more time with the busy college student. I am a big spoon and a big spoon with my love of over 14 years and I love that about us because we are both vulnerable and we are both protective with eachother, this beautiful duality. When I notice my marianismo gems, it makes me grateful for the resourcefulness I conjure up in a pinch and the grateful spirit that was passed down to me through my epigenetics.

NURTURING MYSELF

My Marianismo
mascots

When re-claiming spiritual protection and ancestral attachment connection, consider the ways in which animals have also been colonized with their ecosystems altered by our lifestyle. Consider how animals have adapted and how they can show us about our own inherent gifts.

The English Bulldog is a colonized breed raised for the purpose of bull baiting. Their genes were bred to be violent and aggressive. In the 1700's England finally banned bull fights and the bulldogs were facing extinction. It took bulldog lovers to breed the bulldogs with the most gentle bulldogs in the lineage for generations until the bulldog became epigenetically altered to what is today a top 5 pick for family friendly dogs because they are loving, gentle, and they love to rest. This dog reminds me of our Marianismo epigenetic history of change despite colonization.

Rose
English Bulldog
adopted
Summer of 2023

Spritual Protection: Rose's origin story

True story, I am in the middle of an ancestral retreat in sacred Utuado, Puerto Rico, hosted by Natalie Gutierrez, LMFT and Dr. Lydiana Garcia. My husband was at home with our 3 sons and while I was trying to meditate, connect with my intuition, I was feeling guilty for having such a relaxing time. He said the boys were restless without me and by day 6 he didn't know what else to do to help all of them with the lonliness so he packed up the car and headed to the animal shelter. He said Rose was calm and patient as they looked at all the dogs. He said she had been malnourished. He adopted her and took her home that day.

The thing is, before leaving on the retreat I was feeling in a flow and knew I wanted to plant 3 rose bushes in front of my house and so I did. While Mike was at the pound on a whim, I was participating in an ancestral guided meditation at the retreat. I remember meeting my paternal grandmother at a bench overlooking Progreso Beach. We were both watching my kids play in front of us. She said to me "don't worry mija, even when you're not there, I am protecting your family". It felt like this warmth all over my body and this tranquility. When I checked my phone that evening after a full day of ancestral guidance, I saw Mike's text that he had adopted an English bull dog "she is so sweet, the kids love her and they keep calling her Rosa, like a Mexican grandmother but her name is Rose. We can't wait for you to meet her, you're going to love her". Right then my body said, she's ancestor sent. She loved me on sight and follows me around everywhere I go.

NURTURING MYSELF

My Marianismo
mascots

Excerpt from the book "The Soul of an Octopus" by Sy Montgomery

"Unconstrained by joints, her arms were constantly questing, coiling, stretching, reaching, unfurling, all in different directions at once. Each arm seemed like a separate creature , with a mind of its own. In fact, this is almost literally true. Three fifths of octopuses neurons are not in the brain but in the arms. If an arm is severed from an octopuses body, the arm will often carry on as if nothing happed for several hours. One presumes the severed arm might continue hunting and perhaps even catching prey- only to pass it back toward a mouth to which the arm, is , sadly, no longer attached." page 14.

Reading this except from the perspective of a marianismo mascot with legacy resources and the flexible hard working ability of this brilliant, adaptable, shapeshifter, we honor the octopus as a marianismo mascot.

The Giant Pacific Octopus

The octopus has been a mystery to man for thousands of years and has had folklore written about it. The female Giant Pacific Octopus, however, she is a Marianismo mascot just as she is. She is a magician, a shapeshifter, she in an innovator using whats around the seafloor to create safety, a disguise, a home. From shells to sunken ships she blends into her environment, can create in seconds, and has the gift of hypersensitivity- she can feel more intensely through the cells of her suctions which allows her to become her environment from changing colors to picking up the vibration in the water to find food, she is in flow with her environment and her divine assignment.

How do you identify with the legacy burdens and legacy resources of the giant pacific octopus?

NURTURING MYSELF

My Marianismo
mascots

Q: What are YOUR mascots? What animals have supported you through life in sync of your challenges and a reminder of your shared strengths?

In what ways are animal mascots inspiration of our ingenuity and in what ways is your connection to animals divine flow?

Hummingbirds

Ts'unu'um is the Maya name for 'hummingbird'. Also called colibris, there are several Maya stories and myths about how the hummingbird came to exist. The beautiful hummingbird was sacred to the ancient Maya. They were considered magical beings and represented beauty, agility, and a messenger between the living and the dead.
Hummingbirds can fly forward and backwards, up, down, sideways and upside down, that's a lot of energy for such a small bird. Imagine them swirling around you with the buzz of their fast wings and their messages from ancestor.
Their wings flap so fast that it makes a humming sound which is a co-regulator for our epigenetics when in the presence of this ancestral bird.

Lizards
The Classic Maya may have taken notice of lizards and even mentioned them in their writing. The word for "lizard" in the Mayan language is tolokok.

Lizards are symbolic for many features, including survival, adaptability, good fortune, protection, transformation, and metamorphosis. Lizards are masters of camouflage, which helps them blend in with their environment and avoid predators. This can teach us that adaptability is not just a way to survive, but also a way to thrive in a changing world. Lizards also have other anti-predator adaptations, like venom, reflex bleeding, and the ability to regrow their tails.

NURTURING. MYSELF

THE FOUR ELEMENTS OF MY MARIANISMO

Fire/Smoke

What is your personal connection with fire?

What is your lineage's connection to fire?

What feelings does fire represent for you?

How does your sacred grief and sacred rage move through phases like the ceremony of fire?

Water

Water is our first home in the womb and holds cellular memory of supporting you, touching you, flowing through you.

How are you like a body of water from the depths of the dark ocean to the foam glistening on top of the shore?

How has water been a co-regulator for you and your lineage?

How do you resource your gifts through water like energy?

Land/Earth

Trees, dirt, mushrooms, plants, leaves, and all the ecosystems supported by land and the cellular communication land holds space for is sacred. Sometimes it can feel emotional to truly surrender and accept that the land loves us so much and is always adapting to hold us. We can go to the land and learn from it, be with in, and let it hold us as we rest, reflect, connect, and re-create new paths back to ourselves and back to the land. What does your intimacy with the land look like? How can your inner child joy be found on the land?

Wind/Air

Whether your breath, your story, your song, your wish blown out with a dandelion, or wind sweeping past you on your morning walk reminding you of your sacred time. Have you noticed wind being a motivator, a loving push in the right direction? How are you like wind for others? How does wind rock you in safety?

Energy Words

Chakra- in traditional sanskrit, "chakra" means wheel and it refers to the energy wheels up and down your energy body. These wheels or disks of spinning energy each correspond to certain nerve bundles and major organs. To function at their best, your chakras need to stay open, or balanced. Imbalanced chakras can lead to a host of chronic physical illnesses or mental health issues due to a weak energy body.

Qi or life force energy- in traditional Chinese medicine, vital energy or life force that keeps a person's spiritual, emotional, mental, and physical health in balance.

Prana- is a Sanskrit term that translates to "life force" or "vital energy.". It means "breath" It refers to the universal energy that flows in and around our bodies, believed to be the breath and the sustaining force of life itself.

Reiki is an ancient Japanese medicine technique that uses gentle touch and energy to promote relaxation, reduce stress, and improve overall health and well-being. It's based on the idea that an unseen "life force energy" flows through people and that physical and emotional ailments are linked to imbalances in this energy.
.
Healing Energy over our Marianismo Energy
My intention is to notice our own energy as medicine or poison for our body and mind.

Have you ever been in a good mood, feeling optimistic and confident, and someone comes around and says something negative and your whole body energy changes? Maybe now you notice you are stomping rather than stepping? Maybe your face went from soft and welcoming to stern and dismissive. People's energy can transfer to us like a cellular transmission. Like trees or mushrooms in a forest, we are communicating on cellular energetic levels. So what if we also have this energy stored in our cells from 7 generations back? What if some of this energy blocking our full light is communication form ancestral roots that have old grounding that is no longer keeping us steady?

What if we intentionally shift the energy and clear out the stuck beliefs from the cells and replenish our energy body, our auric field, with our best version of ourselves, guided by our Spirit guides, ancestors, angels and our own divine highest self?

This is a space to reflect on the energy we exchange with each other and the energy we store for our selves and our loved ones. May we have discernment and fluidity to remember not to be attached to anything not of us, and to ground in our innate gifts and inner knowing. This is a moment to create an energy field in our highest most conscious good.

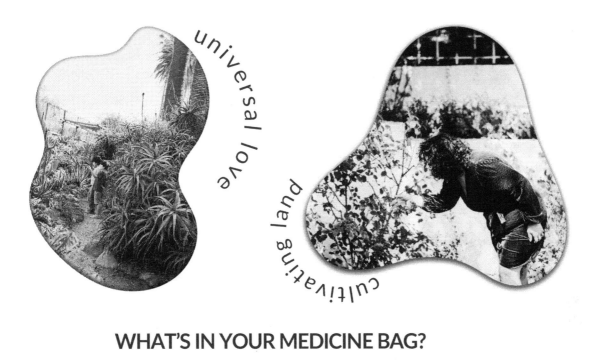

universal love

cultivating land

WHAT'S IN YOUR MEDICINE BAG?
INSPIRATIONAL MOODBOARD & JOURNAL PROMPT

Considering you are the keeper of your magic, you create your own medicine from the mother nature that lives within you and connects to the divine nature we all feel beneath and around us. You are your own apothecary. You gather the cellular strengths of your lineage and your own keen sense of your highest good and you can trust yourself to expand your epigenetic joy. So what gifts or rituals, as medicine or celebration, do you keep in your medicine bag?

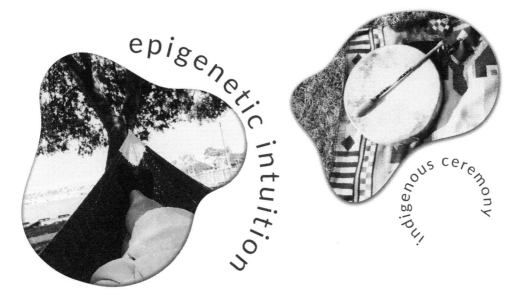

epigenetic intuition

indigenous ceremony

MY MARIANISMO

CAN SHAPE SHIFT AND EXPAND AT ANY TIME, JUST LIKE ME

MY MASCOTS
animals, plants & elements

_____
_____
_____
_____
_____
_____

MY MARIANISMO SACRED ANIMALS

_____
_____
_____
_____
_____
_____

SACRED PLANTS

_____
_____
_____
_____
_____
_____
_____
_____

SACRED CEREMONIES

_____
_____
_____
_____
_____
_____

The Bloom

My Marianismo
Epigenetic impact on The Bloom

The bloom does not just come once a season but rather is always in bloom whether we see it or not. Sure, our bloom is the full rose open to receive the sun's prana energy and that is us in our organic glow, in our discernment, in our sovereignty. When we bloom we make space for the expansive unfurling of our soft petals that represent our experiences that shaped us and became our essence, our heart's bloom, our connection to mother earth and the eco-system that comes to resource us in full bloom and deeply rooted. Once picked we can regenerate for another season of blossoms.

The Bloom can look like
confidence, glowing energy, taking risks, embodying passionate ideas, creating from intuition, self-compassion

The Bloom can feel like
energetic expansion, feeling the collective consciousness, feeling loved, receiving love without pushing away, safety in your body, finally being home, embodying sacred gifts, protection from ancestors

Historical trauma has pruned the bloom only to sell it for mass production. Colonization has limited the abundance of our ancestor's full bloom. Spanish colonization trauma has dettached the rose from indigenous practices distancing the bloom from the roots.

Being in your bloom is indigenous medicine and ancestral reconnection.

The bloom impacts our crown and third eye chakras. Our root chakra is open when we are in bloom.

My Marianismo Epigenetic Hope
The English Bulldog's History of Colonization

Bred for bull baiting from 1210-1835AD (entertainment & profit)

Inbred for agression & fighting until 1800's

Bred to manipulate their looks which has impacted their health

They are 30 times more likely to develop health issues than other breeds

Lower life expectancy

Risking extinction, breeders started breeding the most calm affectionate dogs to save the violent breed from being outlawed

Through epigenetics, English Bulldogs have gone from trauma breeding to #3 most recommended dogs for kids & family

Though their bark isn't loud, they find ways to get their needs met

"Large portions of the bulldog's genome have been altered to attain these morphological changes which has in turn resulted in a tremendous loss of diversity in the part of the genome responsible for normal immune function. The lead author of the study, Niels Pedersen, says that this breed has reached the point where its popularity can't justify the health problems that the typical bulldog is forced to endure and, sadly, not much can be done at this stage."
Smithsonianmag.com

In June 2023 I went to Utuado, Puerto Rico on a spiritual retreat. I was gone for ten days leaving my husband to manage the home w/our three sons. Day 7 I called home & everyone missed me. Day 8 Mike tells me he took the boys top the pound to pick out a dog because they all felt longing & he thought of a dog. "Her name is Rose, a 3 yr old abandoned English Bulldog & the kids love her but they keep calling her Rosa like a n old Mexican Grandma. You gotta meet her." I felt like I already had.

Because of their forced bred strength and viciousness, they were popular in dog fighting as well. The breed almost disappeared when dogfighting was outlawed in 1835 but the breed was saved when owners bred out their aggression.They are now the Top 3 Most Friendly breed.

The thing Mike didn't know because I didn't tell him was:
- A week before the retreat I had an intuitive calling to plant roses in my garden w my mom & chose 3, for the matriarchs.
- The day he got Rose I had gone on a spiritual journey where my Abuela told me "even when you are not with your kids, I am".
- My grandmother asked for una rama de rosas at her altar to remember her.
- I had been avoiding getting attached to another dog since my childhood perrita, Sugar.

She just felt like a loving ancestor. She is a loving presense to everyone. She follows me around.

January 2024 I am at home "homsechooling" my kids & insist they watch an educational movie. I found a dog documentary (I love documentaries) & found myself enthralled. When they brought up the English bulldog I quieted the kids so we could learn the history of our beloved Rose. In stillness with tears down my face learning the colonization and historical trauma of the English Bulldogs, I felt my ancestors had been unraveling this larger understanding with clues & gifts for ME to find to share this information on Marianismo with compassionate examples. This is me and Rose tending to our mission by tending to the collective garden as epigenetic changemakers through love.

Roots to Bloom- A Self Compassionate Body Scan

Working through the bloom of My Marianismo

An invitation to be a loving partner to your marianismo wounds in a way she/they need.

One hand on your heart, another on your tummy or another body part that wants your touch. Big deep breath in as you imagine your breath diving deep into the soil at the bottom of your feet and shooting down to the roots. Exhale as you feel the land holding you, smell the soil, the air has a scent, can you smell it? Visualize the wind blowing you a kiss and as you inhale again you feel the warmth as grandfather sun beams down from your crown and beams golden light through the top of your head through your 3rd eye, unblocking your throat chakra with glittering love. Breathe into the visualization of your heart expanding with the warmth of the sun's prana energy. While your focus is on your heart, allow your heart to tend to your true feelings from the roots to the bloom. Move your body intuitively, as called. Can you witness your process from roots to bloom? If it's too much stop and water yourself in a way that feels good for you. Try again whenever your heart calls.

Can you feel sensations in your physical body or energy body? Can you name the emotion and location in the body?	**Roots: Feelings**
What protectors come to support you? What beliefs do they carry in this situation? What message do they have for me?	**Thorns: Protectors**
What is my expansive epigenetic potential when I am in rest? What was my lineage exceptional at? What are my legacy resources?	**Leaves: Sourced Love**
Being intuition led and in your epigentic flow allows the stem to send the information to the brain and the rest of the body. You are the messenger and the message.	**Stem: Energy Flow**
You are abundant with a disarming fragrance and softness that generations have longed for. What does your blossom feel like? How do you cultivate the environment for your bloom?	**Petals: Soft Bloom**

A loving suggestion: Play "Rose in the Dark" by Cleo Sol while swaying or moving and allow yourself the somatic release your body has been holding.

Here is a qr code for the My Marianismo Playlist to create a space for all the feels

I am the magic of Marianismo- written by Cynthia Alonzo Perez

My Marianismo can fit like a cape that in one swipe of my arm and keeping perfectly silent can help me become invisible. Just like that.

My Marianismo has my Crown replaced with a top hat which others have requested I pull out rabbits and doves for them to marvel at but when I look into it
I see the bottomless portal of endless expectations and illusions

My Marianismo has me pulling compromisos and consejos out of my sleeve like handkerchiefs embroidered and pressed by my tata abuela
My Marianismo has shown my cards to be a seer, a queen, an embodied version of Raquel and her gifts
My Marianismo has made me believe that I am the Magician, the one to perform for everyone and keep them happy and in awe of my many talents
I can move so fast with just a slight of my hand I have turned your tablecloth into a dinner spread

Not impressed? Let me make an ofrenda using only water, fire and my ancestors cellular memory

My Marianismo can wave a wand and just like that, POOF! I'm available, of service, humble af

My Marianismo tells me I must pull more rabbits, juggle more balls, and look exotic doing it

My Marianismo puts me on display everyday to be cut in half and dismembered at my core cells and jammed back together and spun around where my grandmothers womb trauma gets logged in my throat chakra.
And I say thank you,
thank you for allowing me to be cut in half for your applause.
My Marianismo tells me to bow and be humble when the lights go out.
Because I am the magician and the people are waiting

The thing is, I am not the magician. I am the magic. Soy la magica
I carry in my bones the star dust of a night sky that protects the cenotes where my people come from.
I am the wisdom of people who walked on el malecon in relaxation generations before me
I am the magic that can sense in my cells when my children wake up and can see them walking down the hall in my third eye
I am the magic that speaks to you through my visions
I am the magic that has astral-projected here and back to be in the magicians body to perform night after night.

Let me not forget that I am not the magician, but rather, I AM the magic.
I have traded my wand for a drum stick
My cape no longer poofs me invisible but sits on my shoulders like a velvet cloak embroidered with flowers reminding me that my magic is to be protected
My hands are an extension of my heart where humility is vanished into gratitude
My ancestors are the tools to conjure up sacred space for those called
But make no mistake, I am not a magician. I am the MAGIC.

In my Ser, In my Magic

Ser is a Spanish verb that means "to be
Re-imagining my magic as who I am not what I give or how much I carry.
Being in my Ser with the land and it's animals.
Being in my ser and not in a response or reaction
Being in my ser feeling the electrical currents of my cells and lympgatic fluid.
Being in my ser and holding myself with my breaths because I have reawaken to the long for my own touch.
Being in my Ser and not in anyone's projections
Being my Ser and not abandoning myself but reclaiming the women's who's spirits left their bodies long ago and no one noticed because the productivity was met
Being in my Ser, que Sera?

Intuitive
Creative
Connected to Nature
Connected to animals
Connected to the pulse of the collective
Consciousness
Able to give and Receive love without resentment
Protective epigenetics for expansion
Mystical Queen
My ancestors wildest hopes and reawakened dreams
My Ser as an Epigenetic Changemaker
In my flow, in my freedom, I bring ancestor with me

In my Ser on the land
I was called to lead private hammock homecoming meditations in the park, on the land. My grandmother weaved hammocks and huiplies and I realize now she was expressing herself and pouring love into her craft.

Healing Mother wounds in My Marianismo
Root to Bloom
7 week
meditation flow

Root- birthing meditation- womb to bassinet

Sacral- inner child meditation

Solar plexus- animal & self meditation

Heart- opening the heart center with sun & elements

Throat- chants and drum with opening of the throat chakra w prana energy or loving wise ancestor giving expression into throat

Third eye: opening with sun prana energy for abundant wisdom

Crown: opening with reiki healing energy and ancestral protection from benevolent ancestors, guides, Spirit.

This is a meditation flow I host in my groups. This group focuses on healing from marianismo through our life force energy. More information on *"My Marianismo: Energy Healing from Root to Crown"* guided video and workbook on rootedinreflection.org

What would your body and spirit feel like if you were flowing more into your soft epigenetic bloom?

Grace without guilt
Notice without judgement
Listen without answers
Witness without fixing
Recieve without shrinking

Healing Legacy Burdens in Marianismo can look feel like moving
from preoccupied to present
from restless to rested
from Selfless to self loved

Creating My Inner
RETREAT

using cellular resourcing to create inner safety

When thinking about retreating to a place to retreat to that knows you, is always welcoming and safe, remember that you can create that for you and within you using your third eye as "inner resourcing". When you want to ground yourself in your own inner discernment and tranquility, who better than you and your cellular memory of what feels like safety and surrender to YOU? Let's create an inner retreat visualization.

Remembering sacred smoke

I like to imagine myself walking through a portal door (I imagine the door in my third eye and see myself as I am today walking through this door). Once I am through the door I call in a retreat on the land, what the land looks like may change each time or may be the same place every time. Loosely allowing myself to notice and flow with where this visual takes me. Call in a gathering place, a fire pit on the beach or in the middle of the jungle, I know what's best for me. I like to slow down right here and smell and listen. What scents accompany this walk to the firepit? What textures and temperatures do I feel on my skin? What is the weather like and the time of day? I breathe in the call of the fire and allow myself to be present.

Who shows up for me?

When in this sacred space that I have called in within me, I see natural places for others to come and rest around the fire. Maybe they are logs or banana leaves on the sand, either way, when I feel called to, I call in my inner resources to be with me. This could be my consciousness showing me who comes up as a safe person to be here for and with me. This could also be me asking for a spiritual guide to come through. This could also look like you picturing a mentor or loved one as an anchor in this retreat. Who shows up for me? What feelings do I notice? What nuanced and clear messages do they show me through symbolism or an inner knowing?

Tending to my garden

My Marianismo
Epigenetic impact on The Garden

The garden represents the harvest we offer with the epigenetic flow of love, abundance of grace, and embodied ancestral intuitive knowing in ourselves and our ecosystem of family and those in our care. When we embody our truest self, we re-wire our brain and strengthen our epigenetics for our highest evolutionary good. We show up embodied for the love we want to be, it also an example which feels like an invitation to softness and living in our SER, our true self. We have the power to grow a garden 7 generations forward and healing the roots 7 generations back. That is quite the rose garden. Stop and smell the roses.

We all have offerings for the collective garden, some are just at different awakenings and re-births in their life.

"Deja los espacios donde no hay amor"—mi Tia Sara

"Healing is all about creating new neural pathways in the brain to help you respond differently to perceived threats around you. This happens through awareness, practice, and receiving care from people in your community."
— Natalie Y. Gutiérrez LMFT, <u>The Pain We Carry: Healing from Complex PTSD for People of Color</u>

The garden is very much a gathering for multiple co-existing wishes for growth and nourishment. The garden is the lifespan from the seeds of our ancestors to the bloom 14 generations through. The garden is a reflection of cycles below and above the earth as its foundation.

In Season 3 Episode 13 of Confetti All Around Podcast, "Embracing Transitions: The Beauty of the a Death Bloom" we talk about outgrowing our bloom and having to "dead head" to allow for new growth. We talk about the beauty of a succulents and their decade long "death bloom" as it shoots towards the sky in its last grand gesture.

Tending to our garden as healing marianistas might be allowing reciprocity. This could be making a bid for care aka asking for help. This may also be offering support or care when you have capacity and a call to help someone. This can go as deep and timely as standing in your humanitarian marianismo values and boycotting, advocating, resisting oppression for all.

Harvesting our healthy garden gives us a chance to raise the energy we give and allows us time to just be in our bloom, in our bodies, in slowness and sunshine. This is an invitation to center your softness and curiousity. This is an invitation to invite your well and wise ancestors to join you on days that feel hard and for moments that require their apoyo. This is a calling to cut cords from the inherited epigenetic trauma bonds and liberate the ancestors whom we cast away. We can acknowledge stories and circumstances as they happened without taking on the burden.

This last part of this book is our collective garden. I asked the women in this section if they would be interested in contributing to a collective piece on healing marianismo from their own medicina. They all gave a loving yes! These offerings are for you, for others, for future ancestors who may wonder, but how? What are some ways of being a liberated living ancestor? We have been on our journey too and together, we have learned some loving ways to uncover our gifts and witness how lovely we are when we love on ourselves.

Thank you for reading this far and we hope you find something in these offerings to offer your harvest. Con todo cariño.

Community Mothers as a Legacy Resource

This is an invitation to explore within who you can call in as a resource when you feel unseen, unloved, unwelcomed.

This resource can be someone you personally know like an elder or a family friend. Maybe this resource is a your same age or a mentor. Maybe this perosn is someone you never met like an author or painter you admire for their life story and craft. This could be an artist who has passed on but still inspires you.

I find myself seeing my strength and softness through the eyes of my friends, my children, and my community.

My best friend's step mother named Tina has become a dear friend to me and she and I share in vulnerability like friends do. She also holds space for me like a mother when I need it. It feels like I can remember I am loveable withe so many people, not just when seeking my mothers' love.

Authors and artists have shown me nurturing through their stories, words, and stroke of creative genius. I have allowed myself to rest and frolic with the support of the arts and the expansive energy of those who are vulnerable enough to create and loving enough to share it with us.

We can re-parent our mother wounds on the land and under the trees. Sitting under a tree and noticing the animal life that gravitates to you is one way of pouring back into yourself. Sometimes I sit under a tree at my favorite park, the one where I held sessions for three years. There is a man made duck pond and a mile of tall coniferous trees. I sit back and watch the ducks and geese soar overhead and dive into the lake like a ballet. I walk to the path to the large grassy area with few trees where the swallows soar at sunset. If you have never been enveloped by the vibrant energy of swallows buzzing all around you, I highly recommend it. I notice the playful squirrels that are very territorial and often tricksters. I allow myself to ease into being with the land like a great wise ancestor. I ask the land to remind me. I envision my mother's motherland and I allow the feelings to flow up and down from my roots to my crown with gratitude and slowness. I can be a child of La Gran Madre Tierra.

Lastly, I can create community by giving and receiving love. My goal for personal and collective liberation intersect and I can ask for care and I can offer care as I grow my relationship with myself as a loving inner mother, mentor and future ancestor.

7 Daily Rituals for Inner Child Connection

Notice which rituals feel like ease for you and which make your body start calculating the energy it will take. Try not to judge yourself and allow vulnerability and surrender to bring you to the present when in ritual with your inner child.

Intention

What intention do you have for yourself when you wake up? How do you wake yourself up like a loving inner mentor?
Can you start your day with a value to live in for the day? Can you call in 5 things you are grateful for in your life right now?

Delighting

Have you thought of the last time you felt loved in a way that someone simply delighted in loving you just for being? If so and if not, this is a ritual for you to slow all the way down and choose something you enjoy and savor the time and touch. Softening of your face, soothing yourself with kind words helps. Can you frolick today doing only what your inner child delights in?

Rest

This could be literal nap time with a designated cozy spot, this could be stopping in the middle of the park for a forrest stretch & connection with Madre Tierra. This is also creative rest and expansive ideas for what play looks like to you and your inner child. This is whatever rest you need to get back to your core self to be attuned to all your parts.

Creating

This is as nuanced or grand as you feel in the mood for. Creating from your heart space may fill one cup while creating from your 3rd eye fills another.
What do you have within your ancestral lineage that is bubbling up for you to pour out and overfill your life with your creative intuitive expressions?

Discernment

Discernment can feel like discipline or patience in choosing. This is not punishment as it only seeks to self-guide into what is the next best move for your inner child This looks like discerning your role in your day and accountability in a way that re-pairs old violent ways of forcing discipline. How do you teach your inner child a daily flow that honors their soft heart, quirks, and their gifts?

Resourcing

You've been great at re-sourcing your energy and support since you were a kid. It is what kept you literally & figuratively safe when unsafe. This could look like you imagining a loving parent or mentor guiding you through a new transition. This could look like tapping into your grandmother's resources of gardening, business, creativity to source safety when you need it.

Re-Pair

The art of re-pair is important to the inner child who wants to feel seen and validated. Re-pairing old beliefs helps them move past shame in the body and re-wires the inner critic into a more compassionate presence. This could look like journaling, taking accountability, forgiving in a way that is comfortable to you, apologizing to others, and sitting in discomfort with observation.

Which ones will you start with?

Setting your intention, spend a moment imagining yourself in each of these rituals with time, space, and ease.

Inner Child Altars and Rituals

"Okay so you've been doing the inner child things like eating your favorite sour candies or going back to your childhood school for a round of tetherball. But what about getting into an authentic flow with your inner child that is seamless and inviting? I found this hard to find for myself while carving out something as "simple" as making time for my own joy. Rituals felt like selfishness and altars felt like taking up too much space. And that was exactly the medicine I found worked best for me.

It was only in committing to my own inner child rituals and creating the spaces I wished were provided to me as a child, I realized I had this altar within me all along. And the more I cared for this altar with offerings of love and curiosity, the more my inner child showed up for me, easier, with gifts for ME, too. Inner child healing is rooted in indigenous practices that are naturally "polyvagal toning" (strengthening the nervous system to a calm state which widens your capacity to manage stress and be present). This is an invitation to center your loving inner child and the connection you always have with them. " Cynthia Perez, Inner Child Altars and Rituals, free ebook at rootedinreflection.org

Inner Child Altars

When creating your altar, sit in stillness and visualize a place in your surroundings where you can build a soft space for them to come home to. You can clear a drawer, a shelf or even an altar between the roots of an oak tree, for your inner child's altar of curiosity and nostalgia.

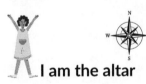

I am the altar
You have a home within, always.
Open your arms & legs out wide and you are the 4 directions & carry the wisdom to guide you.
You have the four elements in your cells and your heart beats in ceremony for you every moment. Call yourself back home.

Altar at home
Where you place your inner child homage is your choice of many as you create a soft space to reimagine your inner child delighting in the offerings you place for them and you. They love this about you and the twinkle in your eye as you recreate autonomy whimsically.

Altar on the beach
Do you like the smooth touch of sea glass? Which shells call out to you?
How can you create a space for your inner child here?
What sea life shows up for you here?

A forest ceremony
Between the trees, under a canopy of leaves and plants in abundance. What kind of ceremony can you conjure up for your loving inner child? What elements support you?

My Marianismo
root to crown
chakra energy shift

Starting at the colors and bodily locations of the chakras, consider where marianismo has blocked your chakras and how you have energy available to you to unblock your chakras and liberate yourself. This ladder is a simple list of what the flow of chakras from blocked to clear may look like on your marianismo energy healing journey.

- **root- trust- safety- home**
- **sacral- guilt- vulnerability- creativity**
- **solar plexus- shame- acceptance- intuition**
- **heart- resentment- forgiveness- joy**
- **throat- fear- expression- authenticity**
- **3rd eye- soul loss- clarity- expansive**
- **Crown- isolation- ancestral wisdom protection**

created by Cynthia Perez for Rooted in Reflection 2024.

NURTURING MYSELF

My Marianismo
rituals
Softening with Self Compassion

Elements: Water or Wind
Chakras: Heart and Root

Observation: Finding it difficult to soften your body to a compliment? Is it hard to receive love from others, or even to believe your own self-love affirmations?

Intention: This intention is to soften your energy body to get to the jelly of your green heart chakra and open it to receive care from yourself and if we practice this enough, we can safely open our chakras to receive care from others.

Invitation:
1. Windy expansion: Best done on a cool breezy day on the land or by the ocean when the wind is flirty. Go to a place where the wind gathers and be barefoot. Picture your inner child playing with this joyful wind energy. See your small toddler self following the snuggly, ticklish wind that holds the moment like a proud ancestor. See your 7 year old self tickled with delight by the winds spontenaity and push of ambition. Witness teenage you on a walk home with the wind guiding you on the safest path like a loyal friend. Welcome back the wind through the palms of your raised hands and swaying of your hips. Mimicking the wind, mirroring this energy like a child jumping into play, let yourself banter with the wind. See where it swoops you up and what it drops you into. Let the elements of surprise and spontaneity of wind swirl around your red root chakra and shake up any stuck susto that has built up stagnant energy.Let the loving movement of the wind flow through your hips and out through your arms as you open them up wide and anchor your four human corners to the divine directions and align with your inner roots.
2. Water memory: This ritual is one for softening up to your own self. This is a shower activity to start or end your day with loving energy. Washing away past self criticism and cleansing the physical body of old negative energy it has had caked on and melted into the cracks. Imagine your body in your 20's. Whether early twenties or later twenties, can you pull up the age in your 20's you were most in survival? With out pulling up the trauma details if you can, pull up a place or an object that represented safety to you at this age. Adjust the temperature and pressure of the water to a comforting level. Using body wash on a loofa or holding the soap bar in your bare hands, work up a lather in your palms while stating your intention for yourself. With a nice lather between your palms, bath your body like that of a loving parent cleansing your 20something body without judgement, with words of comfort and soft touch. Can you talk to your body softly as you touch each part of your body with soap and water and remember the 20something that carried on to get you here? Can you let them know they can slow down, they can soften their approach, they can and will be protected and held by water. Allow the flow of water to re-parent that young adult with softness and a clean slate, ready to receive and already enough to give to thyself.

NURTURING MYSELF

My Marianismo
rituals

moving past regret and into new opportunities

Tools: Visualization & a doorway you walk through often
Chakras: Solar Plexus and 3rd Eye

Observation: Have you been noticing yourself feeling resentful? Maybe there is some regret you find yourself back at and you'd like to stop the spiral and step into your truest most expansive self. Can you make space to create your most passionate, motivated self that finds purpose in getting to be with yourself in this intimate way? What barriers are presently stopping you from stepping into your most real self?

Invitation: This is an invitation to see beyond what your present reality may feel like and to step into the realm of witnessing you frolicking in your purpose and fully in your Ser.
This is an invitation to create portals to your ancient wisdom and personal power.

Cleansing ritual: Without shoulding or judging yourself, find a time to dedicate yourself to sweeping and mopping the main floors in your home. The old saying "pon te a limpiar" to cure depression has spiritual protection that has been exploited for capitalism. Let's think of this cleaning ritual as a moment to set our intention and connect with the wombholders in our lineage that gathered their thoughts here with a broom, a mop, water and their sweat as an offering.

With your sweeping, sweep away any past arguments or stories your ego has been ruminating over. Say something to yourself to remind yourself that you cleanse your space with forgiving and protective love and visualize the broom uncovering and removing old negative energy. When mopping use herbs, plants, and energy cleansing mixtures like florida water, blue anil and camphor spiritual wash, essential oils or fruit peels. Be intuition led and intentional about the protective wash; grounding in your intention and gratitude with each wave of the mop. Call in the energy you want in the home. Call in the way you want your family to feel. Allow yourself to see your family walking on the clean floors and being activated with the love you poured into the home. Each step they take a color shines on them from feet to crown. Allow yourself to hold this imagery of each family member and designated color for each while you mop your home from back to front.

Resourcing & Manifesting My Marianismo shine
Choose a doorway that you want to activate and wipe it down with a cleansing wipe followed by a paper towel infused with spiritual water of your choice (or use lit palo santo and pass it around the doorway with intention to cleanse the space).
Turning this doorway into a portal of peace, hold your heart and take a deep breath and walk through the doorway 3x while you say a loving peaceful affirmation. "All parts of me are welcome here." "Love grounds me here". "I am a portal of soft love". Stand in the other side of the doorway and with your 3rd eye, witness yourself in your most pure authentic love (soak in this visual for a few moments) and ask your heart to remind you of this portal when you are home and in need of a do-over. Remind yourself that you can shift your energy and create a portal back home to yourself every day.

My Marianismo: Music as Medicine

Music has roots in our healing. Not only is music a bridge to language, movement and bilateral stimulation, it transcends time and tradition to offer us a glimpse into the power of soul expression and human craft. African, Indigenous, Spanish, European collaboration of music through salsa, cumbias, boleros, hip hop, etc has sustained our culture with nuances and in lyrics and bold truths through canto. The beat and the instruments carry their own history of colonization and creativity. Music is the first ingredient for most rituals from cooking to cleaning, la musica is the first essential tool. Our bodies remember the hip movement, the stomping, the corridos clearing our vagus nerve. This is our medicina, a portal to the past in the present.

Scan QR code for a curated My Mariannismo Playlist for all the feels.

The My Marianismo Spotify Playlists is a soundtrack to the ebbs and flows of Marianismo. Some of the songs on the My Marianismo playlist:

"Riot" by Summer Walker - In this song Summer sings softly about expecting a relationship to have turbulence to be "love". The marianismo urge to start an argument as childhood norms recreated.

"You said you want love, babe
You said you could give it to me just how I, I need
And you think of roses and daisies
And I think of passion and fire like Hades
You say all the time, peace and quiet
But for my love, I need a riot, a riot"

"Si Te Vas" by Shakira- Oh baby please leave us, not only will we tell you about yourself, we will drag you. Our sacred rage comes through and Shakira's voice is the torch. This song is fuel to burn the anger away and rise the phoenix you are.

"Si te vas, si te vas, si te marchas
Mi cielo se hará gris
Si te vas, si te vas, ya no tienes
Que venir por mi
Si te vas, si te vas, si me cambias
Por esa bruja, pedazo de cuero
No vuelvas nunca más
Que no esta aquí"

"Sabor a Mi" by Edie Gormé y Los Panchos- I love this song for the chords and the tone, the lyrics, however, are questionable. While at a glance the words are lovely, my machismo meter calls bullshit on the "llevaras sabor a mi". When I translate the lyrics in English they read like "gentle machismo" which is still machismo.

"For so long we have enjoyed this love
Our souls have gotten close enough
That I now keep your taste
But you also keep the taste of me
If you were to deny my presence in your life
A hug and a conversation would be enough
I gave you so much life
That by force you now have the taste of me"

"Bonita" by German Valdes "Tin Tan"- This song was chosen by my mother because her father would sing it to her. It was of his time, she would say. I feel a loving and mixed sentiment of fatherly and intimate love blurring. Where your partner is expected to infantalize you or treat you like a fragile doll.

"Bonita como aquellos juguetes
Que yo tuve en los días
Infantiles de ayer
Bonita como el beso robado
Como el llanto llorado
Por un hondo placer"

"Cranes in the Sky" by Solange- This whole album is medicine. The way she describes disassociation and moving away from intuition as a way to cope with these relentless expectations of Marianismo. I can't count how many times I have cried while swaying to this song on repeat until I feel better. Solange is the loving inner mother we need to guide us back to the path of no fucks given again.

"I ran my credit card bill up
Thought a new dress make it better
I tried to work it away
But that just made me even sadder
I tried to keep myself busy
I ran around in circles
Think I made myself dizzy
I slept it away, I sexed it away
I read it away"

"Usted Abuso" by Celia Cruz & Willie Colon- Celia, the abuela of my heart's song. I have so much gratitude for her music and the magic dust she has sprinkled in every song. This one though, she is not going in the shadows or skirting the issue like an obedient femme. She is naming it. You absued me, you took advantage of me, you played games with me and I remember. This is re-claiming self.

"Usted abusó
Sacó provecho de mí, abusó
Sacó partido de mí, abusó
De mi cariño usted, abusó"

"Hasta La Raiz" by Natalia Lafourcade- This song hits all the epigenetic switches like hydraulics on a Cadillac low rider, flashy with the feels. Natalia Lafourcade reminding us of these deep roots.

"Aunque yo me oculte tras la montaña
Y encuentre un campo lleno de caña,
No habrá manera, mi rayo de luna,
Que tú te vayas."

"Rayando El Sol" by Mana- This song is a straight up read of a woman whom is unable to receive love. While many search for her acceptance and praise, they realize it is easier to reach the sun than to reach her heart. I feel these lyrics for the child within longing to be noticed by the divine feminine.

"Rayando el sol, (oh, eh, oh) desesperación
Es más fácil llegar al sol que a tu corazón
Me muero por ti, (oh, eh, oh) viviendo sin ti
Y no aguanto, me duele tanto estar así
Rayando el sol"

"Gift of Life" by Brainstory- I remember where I was when I first heard this song. I was in the matriarch's kitchen whom this song is created after, Tia Naomi, "grandma" to Kevin and Little Tony, 2/3rds of Brainstory. Their grandmother was my husband's maternal aunt and she used to baby sit him as a little chamaco. She gave everyone she loved nicknames and she used to call my husband "Naughty" because one time she pinched his little boy bottom and he pinched hers back! My own sweet memory of Tia Naomi was one of a Marianismo resource. Not only did she always host the annual Christmas party at her home for food and games, she cared for the children. When I was in my deepest post partum fog, I remember her quietly grabbing the baby from my arms and walking him to look at the garden. She knew and never said anything, instead she gave me respite and dignity.

"There will come a time when we'll sing your song again.
So mend us with the winds that send
Seeds of contentment
Leave us with the gift of life."

"Rose in the Dark" by Cleo Sol- If this isn't the song about blossoming from the roots to the bloom I don't know what is! My inner child loves this song sung to them. Cleo Sol's voice is like a loving inner mother reminding us "it'll be alright". This song is perfection.

"I'm a little wiser, baby
I'm a little kinder, baby
After all these years, it's time to let you know
See, I learned some things, my baby
Finally spread my wings to save me
Yes, I lost myself, that's why I had to go"

"Self Love"- by Brittani Williams- This song is, written and performed by a therapist/artist/mc I admire. Brittani Williams, LCSW is the owner of Healmatic, a group therapy practice and she is also a rapper and lyricist. I have co-led two events with Brittani highlighting music and creativity as healing arts and she is not only a beautiful spirit, she is sincere to her craft and watching her perform her song live you see her step into her flow and the impact of her art is a full body feeling. Check out her song on Spotify.

"They be doubting me so much but yo I love me
Self love is the best love yo I love me
Look at the person up in the mirror and say yo I love me.
I'm flawed but hella worthy, dawg I love me."

Confetti All Around Marianismo Episode Resources

This podcast was created out of a need. A need for my own longing to save these healing conversations I found myself having with friends and mentors. The Confetti All Around Podcast is a collection of conversations that highlight the fear and excitement around all of the shifts and everything in between. I could keep writing about Marianismo but Confetti has become a portal to hold space for our ancestral re-connection and inner child repair.

Check out these episodes of Confetti All Around on rootedinreflection.org or on your favorite podcast streaming platform.

Some of Our Most streamed episodes:

#2 with Robin Cortez "Girls Just Wanna Have Boundaries"
#13 Embracing Transitions: The Beauty of a Death Bloom
#4 with Cynthia Perez "Inner Child Healing IS Intergenerational Healing"
#6 with Natalie Gutierrez "Joy is our Survival"
#10 with Maria Lemus Maldonado "Heard and Witnessed"
#12 with Nikolai Pizarro "In Defense of Childhood"
#14 with Denise Silva "She Always Knew, Though"
#15 with Angelica Sievers "The Deeper the Breath, The safer the Body"
#16 with Camara Meri Rajabari "Redefining our Ancestral Genius"
#20 with Sabrina G "I feel Deeply About It"
#21 with Emely Rumble "Inner Child Altars & Book Divination"
#9 with Zina Rodriguez "An Inner Child Beach Day in San Juan"
#17 with Wendy Gonzalez "Hood Honey as Ancestral Medicine

A Bibliotherapy Prescription
from
BIBLIOTHERAPIST MATRIARCH
Emely Rumble, LCSW, Founder of Literapy

"Marianismo, a deeply rooted belief in Latino culture, holds women to the ideal of the Virgin Mary—self-sacrificing, nurturing, and morally pure. While this archetype is often revered, it places immense pressure on women to prioritize everyone else's needs at the expense of their own, leading to higher rates of anxiety, depression, and feelings of inadequacy. " Healing from marianismo involves unraveling these inherited expectations and learning to embrace a more authentic, self-compassionate identity.

Prisca Dorcas Mojica Rodriguez, in 'Tías and Primas', perfectly captures this silent struggle when she writes: "The family matriarch is an interesting archetype within our communities because there are elements of traditional/dominant gender roles that matriarchs enforce and that grant them this status of matriarch. It is often a silent matriarchy that everyone knows is real, but is seldom openly discussed so as not to offend the matriarch's husband, if he is still around."

Reflecting on this, I was reminded of Gabriel García Márquez's 'Until August', where a Latine matriarch approaching fifty begins questioning her identity and desires, separate from her roles as wife and mother. This journey of self-discovery resonates deeply with Dr. Clarissa Pinkola Estés' idea of "gathering the bones" to reclaim the intuitive, wild self—an essential process for healing from societal expectations.

Bibliotherapy—the use of literature for healing—offers a powerful tool for women seeking to understand and break free from the emotional weight of marianismo. Books create a space for self-reflection, helping women trace the impact of these cultural beliefs through generations and empowering them to write their own life script, one based on their true desires and aspirations." --Emely Rumble, LCSW academy.literapynyc.com

Using Bibliotherapy to Understand Marianismo and Its Impact on Women's Mental Health

Book List: Understanding and Healing from Marianismo

1. Like Water for Chocolate by Laura Esquivel
2. I Am Not Your Perfect Mexican Daughter by Erika L. Sánchez
3. Woman Hollering Creek by Sandra Cisneros
4. The House of the Spirits by Isabel Allende
5. The Undocumented Americans by Karla Cornejo Villavicencio
6. Clap When You Land by Elizabeth Acevedo
7. Borderlands/La Frontera by Gloria E. Anzaldúa
8. Mexican Gothic by Silvia Moreno-Garcia
9. The Poet X by Elizabeth Acevedo
10. In the Dream House by Carmen Maria Machado
11. You Sound Like a White Girl by Julissa Arce
12. The Death of Artemio Cruz by Carlos Fuentes
13. Hood Feminism by Mikki Kendall
14. Sab and Autobiography by Gertrudis Gómez de Avellaneda
15. Her Body and Other Parties by Carmen Maria Machado
16. Chronicle of a Death Foretold by Gabriel García Márquez
17. The House on Mango Street by Sandra Cisneros
18. How to Be an Adult in Relationships by David Richo
19. The Souls of Womenfolk by Alexis Wells-Oghoghomeh
20. Feminism Is for Everybody by bell hooks
21. All About Love by bell hooks
22. The Invisible Mountain by Carolina De Robertis
23. Wild Tongues Can't Be Tamed edited by Saraciea J. Fennell
24. Perla by Carolina De Robertis
25. God Spare the Girls by Kelsey McKinney

This curated list offers diverse perspectives on the societal expectations placed on women, helping readers reflect, heal, and reclaim their power—giving us the tools to "gather the bones" and rebuild our narratives.

Curated by: Emely Rumble, LCSW, Author of 'Bibliotherapy in The Bronx'
academy.literapynyc.com.   Order Emely's book for more medicina.

Your Inner Child and the Ancestors
By Rosa Shetty, LCSW

What if you could transcend time and connect with all the abuelitas and elders in your lineage, drawing upon their wisdom and love to help you heal from past wounds? This connection is entirely within reach through the power of your mind and imagination. Healing your inner child with the support of your ancestral lineage is something you can access at any moment, in any place. To call upon this ancestral wisdom, close your eyes and envision the beautiful child within you. See your ancestors encircling this child, showering them with the love, attention, and validation they deserve. If this was missing from your childhood, now is the time to "re-parent" your inner child with the support of those who came before you. Through this process, your inner child can finally feel the safety and protection of a loving elder's presence. I created the following meditation to help you connect with your inner child and ancestors. As you immerse yourself in this meditation, take note of how your energy shifts. Above all, observe with compassion and curiosity, free from judgment. There is no right or wrong—only the act of witnessing, allowing, and accepting whatever arises in the present moment. Let your ancestors step in and assist in the healing of your inner child.

It is my heartfelt hope that this meditation deepens your healing journey. May it provide a gentle, loving space for you, your inner child, and the lineage that supports you.

Meditation exercise on the next page.

Rosa Shetty, LCSW is the host of the podcast Inner Healing Paths and specializes in inner child healing and ancestral healing. She is the author of the book INNER CHILD MEDITATION JOURNAL: 21-Day Guide to Connect With Your Inner Child Daily.

Your Inner Child and the Ancestors
By Rosa Shetty, LCSW

Meditation Exercise:
Find a comfortable spot where you won't be interrupted for at least 10 minutes.

Light a candle and burn sacred smoke such as palo santo, sage, rosemary, incense, or copal.

Close your eyes and say, "This is an offering of love and gratitude to my ancestors. To everyone in my lineage who is well, I invite you to step forward. I welcome you into this moment."
If you prefer, you can do this with an unlit candle. Close your eyes and say, "I light this candle as a symbol of gratitude to my ancestors. I invite you into my life to know you and experience your presence." Then, proceed to light the candle.

After these words, give yourself a few moments—or as long as you need—to settle into silence and begin your visualization.
Close your eyes and take a few slow, deep breaths, grounding yourself in the present moment. Now, imagine yourself as a child. Let any age come to mind naturally. Notice what arises— observe the emotions, colors, temperature, lighting, and any other details around you. Allow your imagination to gently guide you through this experience.

How does this child feel? Are they joyful, anxious, shy, curious, or something else? As the image of this child becomes clearer, see them move closer to you. How do they react to your presence? Are they happy you've come to visit? Do they feel safe and comforted?
Now, imagine telling this child about the ancestors who watch over them. Visualize the moment when you introduce your inner child to your ancestral lineage. As your ancestors gather, see them offer this child all the love, attention, and validation they've always needed. Watch how your inner child responds. How do they feel in the presence of this unconditional love and support? Observe without judgment—witness and allow.

When ready, gently say goodbye to the child and your ancestors. Take a few more deep breaths, slowly returning to the present. When you open your eyes, take a moment to reflect. Write down any feelings, insights, messages, or thoughts that surfaced during your visualization.

Gracias Madrecita

A Generational Love Story by Mayra Najera founder of Gracias Madrecita

I willingly drowned myself in darkness for ten days during a darkness retreat, cutting my umbilical cord from the world. My fear of abandonment hurt me in monstrous ways. Raised by a woman who felt unseen—not only to her husband but to herself—I learned to disappear. If she could be left behind, why not me? Is this why I leave first? To protect myself from being left behind? A whisper found me: "What if this happened in the womb?"

Then, out of nowhere, Gracias Madrecita came to me—a fun, big-hearted little card game to play with your mama. It invites joyful play and discovery for the things we almost forget to say until they're nearly lost, allowing you and your mom to experience each other like it's the very first time. Annoyance boiled over, like my mom's caldo simmering on the hottest days. Was this a distraction? Yet the idea wouldn't leave, bien terca (very stubborn), as if it needed me to create it.

I began to hear the voices of the women who came before me, alive in my mother's womb, waiting to be heard. Marianismo taught me to swallow my words and hush where I might've spilled heartbreaks and dreams. Mama, where's our generational joy?

When the ten days ended, I returned dripping in joy. Instead of drowning in darkness, I found myself dancing and singing a todo pulmón (at the top of my lungs) "Amor Eterno," the song Mi Ma sings to grieve her Mamá, who died when she was five. Suddenly, my knees sank to the floor as I realized that Mi Ma was once a little girl forced to mother her siblings, just like me.

I asked my mom, "Mamá, ¿qué pasó cuando yo estaba en tu vientre?" Her eyes nestled in mine as she shared that mi Papa left to celebrate my upcoming birth. Though he returned seven days later, she felt alone and unloved in a new country. Swimming in her belly, I drank her loneliness and ate her abandonment.

While playtesting the game, I pulled a card: "Mama, is there anything you've always wanted to say to me?" She replied, "I told your sister that I feel like you don't love me." In that moment, I saw my mom as a woman who felt unloved, and I was there to declare that she is lovable.

Gracias Madrecita isn't just a game; it's our medicina—a playful and vulnerable conversation that frees us beyond roles. To those who play, and for those whose moms aren't ready—be open to a 'no' for now. Remember, she is more than just tu Mama—she was once a little girl with her own dreams and fears. Healing takes teamwork—a gathering of ancestors and you, the living ancestor, discovering your generational joy.

To those who play, and for those whose moms aren't ready—be open to a 'no' for now. Remember, she is more than just tu Mama—she was once a little girl with her own dreams and fears, too. Thank you for your curiosity and willingness to heal through play. Healing takes teamwork—a gathering of ancestors and you, the living ancestor, discovering your generational joy.

Gracias Madrecita is a question-driven card game where Mamas and their grown-up kids take turns on a journey of self-discovery.
You are invited to experience the power of being curious, free, and vulnerable in communication.
The purpose is heart-to-heart intimacy, unconditional love, and deep gratitude for the past, present, and future.

Mini Sampler Gracias Madrecita Questions:
- Mamá Asks: Is there a food that immediately takes you back to your childhood with the very first bite? Tell me the story behind it.
- Mamá Asks: If you were younger right now, what would you like to hear from me?
- Child Asks: Mamá, imagine you're a teenager right now. What advice or valuable insight would you share with your younger self?
- Child Asks: Mamá, did you make any conscious decisions to raise me differently than your parents raised you? Why was it important to you?
- What's the story of your greatest love and what made it special? Did it involve heartbreak? How did you find healing?
- If we could magically become kids again right now, what adventure would you like to go on?
- Mamá Asks: Is there a time you changed your dreams or goals to make me proud? How was that for you?
- What is something you've always wanted to ask or say to me?
- What is something that brings you joy that we can explore together soon?

Created by Mayra Najera
www.graciasmadrecita.com

Irelia Ozaeta herbal artisan and owner of Cosmic Rose Apothecary
Uprooted and Blooming – Remedies to help ground, connect, and protect your divine energy

I am Irelia Ozaeta first generation Mexican-American, eldest daughter to immigrant farm workers. I grew up in Salinas, California, which is often called the "Salad Bowl of the World", due to the booming agriculture. I followed the clear instructions set forth by my immigrant parents.
"Ve a la escuela para que no trabajes como nosotros."
I am the first in my family to graduate from college and obtain a master's degree in educational leadership. This is an extraordinary achievement as my parents only have a primary education from a rural town in Mexico. Providing high quality education was my way of paying it forward.

I devoted 17 years of my life to the educational system. From a middle school teacher, to a middle school principal, and concluding my journey as a senior executive in the largest school district in Monterey County serving over 15,000 students.
I had many accomplishments, accolades, and monetary success; yet I was empty, exhausted, and depressed. My spirit was not thriving in a system that had brought me so much societal success.

In 2020, I married the love of my life and relocated to Los Angeles, California. I uprooted and left everything I had ever known. No longer the familiarity of family, friends, career, or home. There was a tremendous ego death that occurred. I was no longer Ms. Dominguez, the highly accomplished educator and community leader. I would often ask myself -Who am I if I am not an educator? What's my contribution to society? This transformational uprooting carried an opportunity for reflection and for something new to blossom. I began to reflect on activities that brought my spirit joy, and engaged in opportunities that would water and nurture my soul. I allowed myself to contribute to humanity in a way that did not deplete my spirit. I began gardening and reminiscing on how much I loved flowers and plants as a child, playing in my maternal grandmother's garden. This revival of my inner child led me to taking herbal courses and traditional Mexican herbal workshops, and immersing myself in work led by traditional healers in a variety capacities. I was volunteering to give community "limpias". I was building community through social media, and collaborating with mentors. I was creating oils, salves, and beauty products that were home grown and hand crafted. This is how **Cosmic Rose Apothecary** came to life. I have embraced that I am now a herbal artisan and business owner who specializes in hand-crafted skin products that exclusively uses ingredients that are healthy, beautiful, and in harmony with Mother Nature. My spirit and inner child have been nurtured through my reconnection to mother nature making me a more resilient flower.

Uprooted and Blooming – Remedies to help ground, connect, and protect your divine energy

As an offering, I would like to share a couple of remedies that can be used to help ground you, connect to your divine energy, and protect your peace.

Grounding by Oiling - Oiling of the feet is an ancient practice that is not practiced as often yet yields tremendous benefits to all that have it as an ongoing practice. Oiling the bottom of your feet in the evening can help ground you. We often live in our mind and have a hard time settling into our body which prevents us from obtaining restful sleep. You can get any type of herbal infused oil; I personally like to use my own lavender oil. You begin by placing about 3-5 drops of oil in your hand and rub them together. Once you have warmed the oil you begin rubbing the bottom of your feet (one foot at a time). Take long deep breaths and close your eyes. This self-care practice is relaxing the nerves at the bottom of your feet and helping you return to the connection with your body.

Connecting & Protecting - Copper is a metal that is native to earth. It is ruled by mother earth and the fire element. Copper is a protective metal that enhances and harmonizes your energetic field. It is a silent helper, helping us connect with our ancestors so we may receive healing. Cooper is a conductor, so it extracts energy and helps amplify the spiritual benefits of any stone or crystal it is paired with. You can wear copper jewelry such as bracelets, rings, or earrings to keep you connected and protected throughout your day.

Clearing - Florida Water is a citrus scented cologne that was popular in 1800's made from citrus and herbs. It remains in popularity with spiritual practitioners because it is easily accessible in most drug stores, yet has the power of herbs and flowers that are beneficial to clearing a space. It is said to remove unwanted vibrations and thought forms. It helps calm a space with too much energy. Use Florida water as a spray to clear your environment. Combine the Florida Water with some distilled water and put it in a spray bottle. Spray the corners of any room. Spray after intense emotions have been displayed in a space. You can also directly add some Florida Water to your hands and rub them together. Then brush your damp hands in a sweeping motion towards the ground. This will help clear away any energy that may have attached to you, making you feel irritable or drained.

*Irelia Ozaeta is a talented herbal artisan and owner of
Cosmic Rose Apothecary. A small woman owned business, that
focuses on creating natural remedies and skin products that are
healthy, beautiful, and in harmony with Mother Nature.
To learn more about natural herbal skin care, herbal remedies,
as well as protective jewelry.*

*You can follow her on Instagram @cosmic_rose_apothecary
and on TikTok @cosmicroseapothecary*

Ancestors Mama on Marianismo

Marianismo depends on the co-dependent dynamics found in many Latino families from the roles and duties required of women, and their worth dependent on how they meet those requirements.

So much of our voice is silenced when it comes to our needs and desires unless it pertains to the needs of others. Our emotional safety is minimized, as unnecessary for the survival of these cultural cycles to continue as the norm.

Eventually, our voices become filled with rage, to fight for the justice we didn't receive. Sacred Rage is the rebellion that lives in our veins through our ancestral voices demanding reparation! It is a battle many chain breakers face, to change the harm done by these dysfunctional dynamics.
Many of us go through this journey alone condemned with ridicule from our family. Yet we know we must fight on to free our lineage from this perpetual pain of belittlement and smallness.

Marianismo teaches us from these very real lived experiences that we must be small, meek the good girl to receive love, and thus our relationship to receiving love is tainted. Eventually, the fire seeking justice for our pain dampens, and we have nowhere to go but inward.
This work is for the strong who refuse to accept things as they are because "that's how they've always been." We know deep beneath our bones before we even had to language to explain this knowing it cannot go on!!

Leaning on our benevolent ancestors who have answered the call of doing this work beside us, is key at times when we feel like we have no support! For many of us chain breakers are the black sheep, who become ostracized refusing to carry on with the dysfunction that runs rampant.
But even sacred rage has its time in closing, every cycle has death waiting at its doorstep to welcome a new direction. The fire runs out because what fueled it was only anger, and anger only lives in the absence of love.

While action out of sacred rage was filled with self-preservation, the act of witnessing our neglected needs with warmth and embrace is what carries us forward! Action without our witnessing are empty promises, made in the hopes we will do things differently.

All fires are blown away by the dark cold nights, and it is in this cold silence we find the true wisdom to move on with love's embrace! It is in the whispers of our ancestors we find the peace to accept & expect not everyone is meant to be on this journey alongside us.
In the secret knowings of our heart, we find that dependency on others' will to change is their own; not ours to control. And by that release, we realize we too must let go of these heavy expectations that were only met by disappointment.

Ancestors Mama on Marianismo

Our freedom from these toxic ties requires the fortitude and strength to reclaim our power for our own safety. Moving analytically will never change the minds of those who benefited from our demise.

For this reason, we are led by the ways of our ancestors, where words can only touch the surface of the medicine that lives in us all. It is through the bodily recognition we can then begin to weave this embrace of strength and softness.

Through our womb, we can feel all the ways our abuelas before us, created this space for our safety and belonging. Through our emotional bodily knowing, we receive gifts of insight and healing.

Thus it is through this bodily knowing our emotions paved the way to our redemption in reclaiming this autonomy that was always our sacred rite!

I channeled my "Marianismo No Mas" Oil from this inner journey with my matriarchial Medicina Mujeres, who guided me along this path. I also created other oils Like the Wild Woman, my Banish, and Ancestors Oil to further help along this journey each step of the way! I truly believe we hold the wisdom and medicine of generations in our blood and bones, and some things are too sacred to be explained other than what we hold inside as sovereign beings!

Some other herbs to help along this journey:

Cinnamon for warmth in times of solitude

Marigolds for remembering our magic, when joy seems to be absent

Ruda/Rue to protect and envelope our ancestral knowingness

Angelia Santiago aka Ancestors Mama
ETSY BOTANICA: https://www.etsy.com/shop/AncestorsMama?ref=seller-platform-mcnav
Website: https://ancestorsmama.podia.com
Substack Newsletter: https://ancestorsmama.substack.com/
Tik Tok: @ancestors_mama
Threads: @ ancestors_mama
Ancestors Mama Podcast;

Marianismo & Ancestral Medicine by Veronica Rodriguez Cabrera

Ancestors play an important role in our lives that is interconnected to our healing. Ancestors include our revered family members in our blood lineage that have passed away but who continue to play an important role that can provide strength/soul energy, guidance, assistance and love. Who is considered an ancestor has to do with blood lineage but also is able to extend outside blood relationships and may include sacred land and honorary ancestors (Buenaflor, Erika. Veneration Rites of Curanderismo.,18). Sacred Mesoamerican indigenous teachings share that the soul energy of ancestors continues to flow into their descendants. Honoring and working with our ancestors can give us opportunities to heal ourselves, our family and ancestors. **Ancestral medicine integrates indigenous knowledge and practices when healing ancestral trauma wounds. Building a (re)connection with our ancestors through holistic practices, rituals and ceremony is important in healing ancestral trauma.** Ancestral medicine is also connected to our physical body which is a source of information and ancient wisdom.

Marianismo intersects with ancestral work through our understanding of the epigenetics and cultural and family legacy burdens that we carry. (Gutierrez, Natalie.The Pain We Carry. 29). Some of our ancestors experienced cultural and familial legacy burdens though experiences of personal abuse, economically empoverished, conditions of war, genocide and colonization which has been not been fully acknowedged and witnessed. Our ancestors carried cultural legacy burdens from harmful and oppressive systems which imposed systems of beliefs and values that impacted them and future generations. These ancestors are energetically burdened by unmet needs. Family legacy burdens are deep wounds that can come from harm done to ancestors but also if ancestors perpetuated harm.

In epigenetics, **trauma bonding somatic experiences leave traces on our minds, bodies, spirit and also impact the people around us** (Van De Kolk, A Bessel.The Body Keeps a Score.). In epigenetics, considering our ancestors who experienced harm and who may have themselves done harm, trauma effects linger in our bodies and get unconsciously transferred to our children. We carry our families and ancestral gifts but are unable to fully access or express them due to ancestral wounds. This can lead to unconscious patterns that play out a role we step into in our family system.

In Marianismo and Family Constellations, exists imposed expectations that are embedded in our personal and ancestral stories that have also been woven and encoded within our bodies, minds and spirits. These beliefs, ideas and old stories can be a manifestation of an ancestral burden and also a collective wound and legacy burden. Through colonialism, oppressive systems distort truths that change the fabric of our reality, influenced by patriarchal colonial cultural narratives that are actively taught through indoctrination. Living in a post modern time, we are searching for connection and recognize the importance of healing with our ancestors.

Marianismo & Ancestral Medicine by Veronica Rodriguez Cabrera

Family Constellation is a modality that offers an opportunity to reconnect with our ancestors and heal ourselves, our family and our ancestors. Family Constellations can open an ancestral line of communication that gives you a larger picture of core family patterns. **There are three main principles in Family Constellations which include Order, Balance and Belonging.** Order speaks to an understanding of elders as who came before us, such as our parents, elder siblings and ancestors. In order, there is also an acknowledgment that elders have accumulated more experiences of wisdom and generally have more to give to their future generations. In Balance, it is the act of giving and receiving; reciprocity in family relationships. Belonging speaks to our right to belong to our family system. When these needs are not met, over time it can cause maladaptive patterns in future descendants such as Marianismo.

Marianismo shows up in Family Constellation as an invitation to see core hidden dynamics that have been carried by our parents and ancestors. There is a family and ancestor wound that is connected to a collective wound such as colonialism. Colonial systems have and continue to be a source of disconnection to self and each other. Family Constellations centers inclusiveness and invites our healing intentions which open up sacred intuitive movements within our body. We begin to sense a memory stored deep within your consciousness that is part of our larger family system and legacy. This visceral way of receiving information via our body sensations catalyzes deep resonance. It brings subtle movements from within our system which ripples extend to family and ancestral relationships (Nyaki, Efu. Healing Through Family Constellations & Somatic Experiencing. 50). Setting an intention to heal with ancestors initiates a sacred movement. The sacred movements begins to activate cell memories that unfold our system so we can acknowledge what is wanting to be seen for deep healing.

Acknowledgement is the action that allows us to see what has been hidden within a family and ancestral lineage. Acknowledgement supports our ability to consciously heal ourselves, family and our ancestors. We acknowledge the roles and dynamics that we inherit from our parents and ancestors so we can release ourselves from stories and roles that do not belong to us (Hilenger, Bert, Loves Hidden Symmetry. 5). Through acknowledging what is, we can accept the truth of what has happened. Acknowledgement and acceptance does not mean forgiveness, rather this allows space to witness and acknowledge what is. When we are able to truly witness and acknowledge, we can step into a space of surrender and trust within. This process allows our system to come forward and show us what has been deeply hidden. Offering an opportunity for our ancestors to reclaim their stories and lost parts. Giving us an opportunity to reclaim our stories and reclaim and redefine our beliefs and values. This helps us to fortify and strengthen our roots, ourselves and family.

Marianismo & Ancestral Medicine by Veronica Rodriguez Cabrera

Recommendations when working with Marianismo and mother wounds is letting go of judgement and leaning into curiosity. Healing statements are spoken as part of the movement of acknowledgement, gratitude for your life which initiates a release of old stories that do not belong to you. Ancestors will pick up their burdens and you release the ancestral burden that you were unconsciously carrying. In this movement, when we are able to consciously accept our ancestors, we receive their love fully. This is an acknowledgement of the life that was given to you.

What can be helpful in working with Marianismo and ancestral wounds is to remember that these imposed roles and old stories may be our families' and ancestor's stories, but we get to have our own stories. Reconnect with your ancestors and open and deepen a flow of love that will support your authentic growth and alignment. **Let us reclaim our ancient stories, beliefs, values and rituals. May we release oppressive old stories and patterns that do not serve us in order to move closer to our true essence and our personal and collective liberation.** As we redefine our relationships with ancestor, family, self and beyond; boundaries are a necessary part of our healing journey.

Boundaries are not negative and may be how we learn and practice moving towards being in right relationship with each other. They involve developing an authentic relationship with self and others. Boundaries are less about keeping things away instead teaching us how to be in right relationship with each other. Ancestral medicine is potent and important to meet yourself at your capacity. Ancestral medicine comes from within. We tap into ourselves to look deeper into hidden truths that are stored in our bodies. Ancestral healing involves deep shadow work as it faces you with any truths that have been hidden to you. This may be generations of ancestors who may have not been able to heal their wounds while in their incarnation on earth. Lastly, I recommend play. Allow yourself to have time to find play. Reconnecting to ancestors will reconnect you with your mind, body and spirit. Creating time to play and nurture your body is part of this reclamation work. Inviting joy into our daily lives as we heal our ancestral and collective trauma wounds is part of the medicine we carry. Reclaiming ancestral joy is one of the ways we can integrate healing movements, such as in a Family Constellations circle. Feeling the flow of love pass down from generation to generation as it moves towards you is a powerful opportunity to receive from what is destined for you. **Through this work we engage in the natural flow of nature and reclaim our ancestral medicine.**

Veronica Rodriguez-Cabrera is a Licensed Clinical Social Worker residing in the San Gabriel Valley, aka Tongva land. She identifies as Xicana/indigena mujer who has spent most of her career in mental health working with children and families, adolescents, adults, couples, groups and working in systems. "I am rooted in the four directions and center my work as mami, healer and community member supported and guided by spirit. My daily practices are grounded in gratitude and honor the elements; land, water, fire and air."
For more check out Confetti All Around Season 2 episode 14 & 15 with Vero
Work with Vero at
www.veronicarodriguez-cabrera.com for private or community constellations
IG:Vero_c77

My Marianismo Memes

Doing the work to clear my ancestor's burdens by living in my radiant joy is my expansive purpose.

ROOTED IN REFLECTION

When I set a boundary that keeps me aligned with my personal values, I am doing intergenerational work my ancestors acknowledge with abundance.

ROOTED IN REFLECTION

When I meditate on the land, my crown is open and eager to receive messages for my highest good.

When I step into my gifts from my lineage, I unlock my full potential and purpose.

I am the storyteller for my family.

I can hold space for their stories.

ROOTED IN REFLECTION

When I pause and tap into my inner ancestor, I am proud of the wisdom that spills out of me.

ROOTED IN REFLECTION

Me when I finally answer my ancestors' call and go back to my ancestral land ready to rest and learn.

ROOTED IN REFLECTION

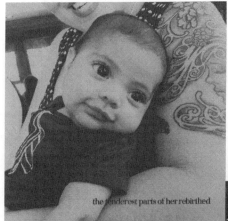

I found this 4 lined post with these photos in my drafts. I do not remember making these but I love past me for these rituals of gratitude.

My first baby, we really saw all of eachother and have felt deeply about eachother since.

Idris and I knew we were gonna be family from the first time we met. He had this inner light like the only star in the sky. I got to be a friend and parent to him and that is a privilege. This is us dancing at the after party of a small off broadway play we both performed in that night called "Shadows".

This photo is at a family member's baby shower where I was having post partum anxiety about being out alone as a new mother. Tia Naomi held my son while I got some time with myself. I still remember feeling cared for by the whole way she was with us.

My little loves are 19 months apart and we call our time together "mother and brothers" (they chose the nickname). We like to go on adventures or to our favorite usual spaces like the library or here at the USC Rose garden and then the Natural History Museum next door followed by lunch at Chichen Itza at Mercado La Paloma.

Disfruta, Hija

One thing I have been suggested to do by my ancestors and spiritual healers is to "disfrutar". To enjoy, to savor the tastes, notes and seasons of my life.

I have this ritual lately that is rooted in gratitude.
"Hijo, the first ingredient in cooking is music!" Me to my 7 & 8 year old sons who has taken a love of cooking and tasting cuisine. I initiate them into the kitchen with Tias Celia & Selena.

I love to think up a meal to make my family. I think of what I have in the fridge and pantry and let myself consult my altar. I take my time letting the ideas come to me and call in some ancestral chef advice from my vast access to extraordinary chefs and creatives.
I make cooking a ritual of gratitude for all the ingredients I have to feed my children. I lovingly acknowledge the times in my genetics my ancestors did not have enough to give their children. I think of my grandmothers that after feeding multiple generations sat down with simply a tortilla to sop up the scrapings left in the pan. I talk to those women while I cook and they have advised me to eat while I cook as a way of nourishing myself intuitively as I go. That way I will have eaten enough by the time it is time to ration or serve the meal to everyone. This is a loving knowing I find myself doing with an ease and a dance in my spirit. It's a gift to unlock this connection with my fellow cocineros and cocineras. I even feel my masculine energy in the kitchen that wants a hearty meal with bold flavors. I let my ancestors cook through me while playing boleros antiguos. When I can, I try to cook meals indigenous to Yucatan and eat tropical fruits that my ancestors enjoyed like pitaya, sandia, limones, naranja agria, guava, mango, piña, y cocos.

One simple breakfast I make to be closer to them is one for the busy matriarch. It is vanilla bean greek yogurt or avena or cottage cheese (whichever I have), sliced fruits like papaya, mango and fresa with honey, cinnamon, chia, and pepitas on top. Grab my coffee and I am grounded in my intentions for the day. Nourished and nurtured I can give back to my family what I give myself.

My own ritual has become, serving my family, curating each bowl for them because I know who likes no meat, who wants extra meat, who likes the rice plain and how many of us are having pepino con limon.

I serve them everything at the table down to the fork, water and napkin and with my grandmother's marianismo love, I do it with an energy of gratitude and affection. And I spend a moment watching them cool down the broth or take the first bite of their crispy taco and I savor their joy. Then, I go to the kitchen and make myself a small sample size of everything. I consider this time like the behind the scenes of a kitchen with several chefs and I honor them by standing in my kitchen at the counter and I taste the food and talk to them about the notes and the layers of flower. "Wow the cumino really elevated it. It didn't come out too spicy like I feared. I'm glad I added the rice at the end. next time I will try it as a caldo", etc. It's like I spend time as the kitchen help in the most intimate and proud ritual of honoring my ancestral support and innovation.

Disfruta, hija

Bibliography

Afro-Mexicans: Illuminating the invisible from past to present: School of Liberal Arts at Tulane University. Tulane University School of Liberal Arts. (n.d.). https://liberalarts.tulane.edu/magazine/spring-2021/afro-mexicans

Boring, Francesca Mason. Connecting to Our Ancestral Past. Healing through Family Constellations, Ceremony, and Ritual. North Atlantic Books. 2012.

Buenaflor M.A., J.D., Erika. Veneration Rites of Curanderismo: Invoking the Sacred Energy of Our Ancestors. Bear Company. 2023.

Dana, D., & Porges, S. W. (2020). Polyvagal exercises for safety and connection: 50 client-centered practices. W.W. Norton & Company.

Estes, Clarissa Pinkola. (1992) Women Who Run with Wolves. Rider.

Guerrero, Diana. (2019). In the country we love: My family divided. GRIFFIN.

Gutiérrez Natalie Y. The Pain We Carry: Healing from Complex PTSD for People of Color. (2022) New Harbinger Publications, Inc.,

Hellinger, Bert, . Love's Hidden Symmetry: what makes love work in relationships/ by Bert Hellinger with Gunthard Weber & Hunter Beaumont. Zrig, Tucker & Co., Inc. 1998.

Lara-Cinisomo, Sandraluz, et al. "Perinatal Depression Treatment Preferences among Latina Mothers." Qualitative Health Research, U.S. National Library of Medicine, Feb. 2014

Medina, Lara & Gonzales, Martha R. Voices from the Ancestors. Xicanx and Latinx Expressions and Healing Practices. The University of Arizona Press. 2019.

Bibliography

Mullan, Jennifer. (2023). Decolonizing therapy: Oppression, historical trauma, and politicizing your practice. W. W. Norton.

Nyaki, Efu. Healing Trauma through Family Constellations & Somatic Experiencing: Ancestral Wisdom from the Snail Clan of Tanzania. Healing Arts Press. 2023.

Rodriguez, P. D. M. (2024). Tias and Primas: On knowing and loving the latinas who raise us. SEAL.

www.sacredearthjourneys.ca/blog/exploring-maya-cosmology/

Taylor, A. G., Goehler, L. E., Galper, D. I., Innes, K. E., & Bourguignon, C. (2010). Top-down and bottom-up mechanisms in mind-body medicine: Development of an integrative framework for Psychophysiological Research. Explore (New York, N.Y.).

https://www.ncbi.nlm.nih.gov/pmc/articles/PMC2818254/

Van De Kolk, A Bessel. The Body Keeps a Score. Penguin Books. 2015.

Work with me
COLLECTIVE HEALING

I am first gen Xicana therapist with 15 years of field work throughout Los Angeles, CA. Cynthia visited homes from the 405 to the 101 to the 10 past the 710 up until the 605. That's a little California humor because this city is vast and diverse and that is what I noticed that our stories as Black, Brown, Indigenous, Queer, marginalized people, we had similar mother wounds and carried deep internalized colonialism within us. I also felt called to go deeper in Marianismo wounds as a full bodied approach to inner child healing for the indigenous colonized inner child and focus on the ancestral attachment trauma through the lens of Marianismo, the mother wound caused by the colonization of Spanish and the forced indoctorination of Catholicism. This is where our stories got lost in the entangled roots but our bodies are waking up.

My calling with Rooted in reflection is to wake up these roots with you in a soft yet intuitive approach that is rooted in my ancestral wisdom, spiritual energy, and my background in therapy as a space holder for trauma. I allow myself to be fully embodied with all my tools for what you are calling in to receive.

Holding Space & Storytelling

I find myself declaring my first role as a creative. This is not a role I used to say with a small voice and last on my list but since embodying this inner child work myself I have unraveled that in many ways of expressing it, I am a story teller.

I started the podcast **Confetti All Around** as a message from my ancestors as a portal to hold space for the cuentos y encuentros of the guests called to share. The podcast highlights our inner child joy and our ancestral knowing.

I am accepting opportunities for paid public speaking, hosting, panel expect and consultation.

Trainings and CEUS

We have 5 CEU Courses rooted in Epigenetic expansion and restorative justice. Sponsored by LatinxTherapy, we offer up to 17 CEUs. We host private trainings and accept Sponsorship.

email us at cynthia@rootedinreflection.org

rootedinreflection.org

Work with me.
1:1

I am first gen Xicana therapist with 15 years of field work throughout Los Angeles, CA. Cynthia visited homes from the 405 to the 101 to the 10 past the 710 up until the 605. That's a little California humor because this city is vast and diverse and that is what I noticed that our stories as Black, Brown, Indigenous, Queer, marginalized people, we had similar mother wounds and carried deep internalized colonialism within us. I also felt called to go deeper in Marianismo wounds as a full bodied approach to inner child healing for the indigenous colonized inner child and focus on the ancestral attachment trauma through the lens of Marianismo, the mother wound caused by the colonization of Spanish and the forced indoctorination of Catholicism. This is where our stories got lost in the entangled roots but our bodies are waking up.

My calling with Rooted in reflection is to wake up these roots with you in a soft yet intuitive approach that is rooted in my ancestral wisdom, my spiritual energy, and my background in therapy as a space holder for trauma. I allow myself to be fully embodied with all my tools for what you are calling in to receive.

Coaching/ Mentoring

Spots are limited due to my availability but I loved the intimate work of 1:1 for those who want to go deeper in a soft and whimsical way.

- 6 session bundles with pdfs and weekly resources in person or virtually

- 1x a month mentorship "pick my brain" calls

- Professional consultation for inner child healing or marianismo work

These offerings range from $300-$3,000 and are NOT therapy but do support your spiritual, physical emotional and professional wellness.

Indigenous Restoration Ceremonies

I am happy to offer intimate 1:1 or small group private ceremonies on the land or by the water. There are a few ways I hold space but each ceremony is unique to the intention and energy you are calling in.

-Inner Child Homecoming
-Womb Healing Hamaca Ceremony
-Inner Child Altars and Rituals
-Intergenerational Healing Ceremonies

email us at cynthia@rootedinreflection.org

rootedinreflection.org

Made in the USA
Columbia, SC
12 November 2024